CONTENTS

I0569949

TRULY MOTIVATIONAL
BASKETBALL
STORIES
FOR KIDS

250 FUN SPORTS FACTS INCLUDED

20 OF THE MOST INSPIRATIONAL TRUE TALES FROM BASKETBALL GREATEST FOR YOUNG READERS & ACHIEVERS

ETHAN WILSON

INTRODUCTION

Get ready to embark on a journey of triumphs, setbacks, and the indomitable spirit that defines the world of basketball. In between these pages you'll discover stories that transcend the court, tales of perseverance, teamwork, and the unwavering pursuit of achieving one's dream. This isn't just a book about basketball; it's a chronicle of individuals who defied odds, shattered expectations, and emerged as legends.

You'll meet Ben Wallace, the first undrafted player to etch his name in the prestigious NBA Hall of Fame. His story sets the stage for a riveting exploration of the game's history, from the powerhouse San Antonio Spurs of the 2000s to the unparalleled dominance of the Chicago Bulls in the 1990s. Brace yourself for the inspirational journey of Kobe Bryant, who overcame early challenges to ascend the ranks to acquire legendary status.

Discover the resilience of Diana Taurasi, rising from humble beginnings to carve her legacy in the WNBA. Earl Boykins, at 5'5", defied the odds, proving that stature is no barrier to success. Join us as we delve into the victories and community impact of the Connecticut Sun and the Minnesota Lynx, before witnessing the awe-inspiring dominance of the UConn Women's Basketball Team.

You'll witness the incredible rise of LeBron James, the rivalry between the Boston Celtics and the Los Angeles Lakers in the 1980s, and the unmatched playing style of Kareem Abdul-Jabbar. The stories don't stop there; explore the success of The Los Angeles Sparks, the global impact of Yao Ming, and the charisma of Shaquille O'Neal.

Prepare to be enthralled by the journey of Dirk Nowitzki, who went from Germany to NBA superstardom, and the unyielding spirit of players like Tim Duncan, Muggsy Bogues, and Giannis Antetokounmpo. Finally, bask in the glory of iconic teams like the Phoenix Mercury in the WNBA.

These tales are not just about basketball; they're about life, passion, and the pursuit of excellence. Whether you're a fervent fan, an aspiring athlete, or someone seeking motivation, this book is your invitation to witness the power of determination and the limitless potential within us all.

So, lace up your mental sneakers, brace for the jump ball of inspiration, and let the games begin.

Everyone's journey in life is different, but many stories start off the same. Like most in Lowndes County, one of the poorest in Alabama, Ben Camey Wallace wasn't born with access to many much-needed resources required to live comfortably. The tenth of eleven children and the last of eight boys, Wallace and his siblings struggled and scraped to make ends meet.

As a family, they would work at the local pecan farms and cotton fields to earn money for the basics. That hard work kept Wallace grounded and close to his family, as he noted in an interview with Sports Illustrated (SI) in 2021, "One or two wrong turns where I'm from could put you on a path that's hard to reverse... We had to stick together to get through."

Wallace's eldest brother, James McBride Sr., played a huge role in supplying the glue that kept the brothers bonded. Wallace remembers the day that his big bro came home with basketball uniforms he'd purchased from a thrift store. McBride Sr. told young Ben that he was forming a team that would play against others in the neighborhood, and just like that, Wallace's life was put on a course that would lead him to become one of the greatest that ever played the game.

As the youngest brother on the court, his older siblings often overlooked Wallace. They didn't want to pass him the ball as they saw him as the weak link in the chain. Determined to prove them wrong, Wallace began to work on what he knew he could control: his speed.

Wallace recalled in the same SI interview, "If I wanted to see the ball, I'd have to get a steal, a rebound, or save the ball from going out of bounds." His brothers actually did him a favor by ignoring the younger Wallace on the court. Instead of sulking, getting mad, and trash-talking, he chose to buckle down, work diligently, and make his presence known.

At the time, his only goal was to dominate his brothers, who underestimated his grit and fortitude. Wallace began to learn the ins and outs of the game and developed a great appreciation for fundamentals. The work ethic he cultivated proved to be his key to success, as it was the force that kept him motivated on the rough road ahead.

After Wallace had accomplished his first goal (silencing his brothers on the hardwood), he was ready for the next challenge, which would find him face-to-face with an NBA legend.

The summer before his junior year, Charles Oakley (affectionately referred to as Oak) rose to fame with the New York Knicks and held a basketball camp in York, Alabama. Although it was a little over 100 miles away from his hometown of White Hall, whose population was about 800, Wallace searched his mind to find a way to make it there. His eureka moment came when he got the idea to offer $3 haircuts to everyone and anyone.

Not unaccustomed to working hard for a dollar, Wallace put his plan into motion. Soon, he would earn the $50 entrance fee required for the camp's week-long experience.

The 15-year-old Wallace would learn many valuable lessons during his stay at Oak's camp. One major lesson came when Oakley challenged him to a one-on-one game. Unbeknownst to Wallace, Oakley was watching him during one of the sessions and noticed that Wallace was bored and not paying attention. Oakley had the remedy to fix that issue.

Known for being an aggressive defensive player, Oakley did not hold back during the one-on-one game. Oakley, who stood four inches taller and at least 50 pounds heavier than the younger player, split Wallace's lip open during a drive to the basket.

Wallace recounts his response to Oak's brutal force in an interview with *Pistons Talk*. After wiping the blood from his lip, the 15-year-old asked Oak, "That's how you play?" According to Wallace, Oak just looked at him and told him to play ball and stop being a punk. On the next play, Wallace drove to the basket and gave Oak a taste of his own medicine.

When Oak asked Wallace if he was just going to "... boom me in the face like that?" Wallace gave Oak the same retort he'd received. Wallace gained Oakley's respect after telling the NBA legend to shut up and ball. An important bond was formed that would later help propel Wallace to the heights of stardom.

In an interview with *SLAM* magazine in 2020, Wallace spoke about Oakley's influence over his game. "He showed me how physical the game of basketball could really be. He showed me a way that I can bring that football nature to basketball, and I took it from there and ran with it." The pair kept in contact with one another after camp ended.

The pivotal meeting of the two future Hall of Famers would be a major catalyst in Wallace's collegiate and professional career. Although Wallace didn't have the grades to get into a four-year Division I university, Oak was able to pull some strings, and Wallace eventually played his junior and senior seasons at Oak's alma mater, Virginia Union.
He led the team to regular season and conference titles in his senior year. Wallace was also crowned the CIAA tournament MVP. Undoubtedly, the ardent defender was getting attention from NBA scouts around the country.

The summer following his junior season at Virginia Union, Wallace and a few teammates stayed in Richmond to further polish their skills and wow scouts sitting in the stands. Wallace was a beast on the court when he returned to play the next season. Virginia Union went to the NCAA Division II Final Four that year. Wallace was chosen as the NABC Division II First Team All-American.

Despite these accolades, the Boston Celtics were the only team to invite Wallace to work out prior to the 1996 NBA draft. The workout didn't go well as the head coach, ML Carr, decided it was best to play the strong man on the perimeter. Carr was not confident that Wallace could hold his own in the paint due to his smaller size.

Still undeterred, Wallace waited for the big day to arrive. Still, his diligence was not recognized when it did, as he went undrafted. What would've broken the spirit of many with hoop dreams served as inspiration for Wallace. He never quit, no matter what anyone around him thought.

It was a lesson he learned early in life back in White Hall, Alabama. When others count you out because of your size or their perception of your abilities, keep your nose to the grindstone. A consistent, solid work ethic can carry you from the depths of despair to the heights of superstardom. All you need to do is believe in yourself, and those around you in a position of power will recognize and reward your efforts.

And Wallace was generously rewarded once he bulldozed through the NBA's door and had the opportunity to put his defensive dominance on display. A four-time defensive player of the year and 2003-2004 NBA champion, Wallace proved all his naysayers wrong.

In 2021, Big Ben received the highest honor given in professional sports. His induction to the Naismith Hall of Fame was the pinnacle of a career born from the sheer strength and resolve of a little brother who wouldn't be ignored. Not only did White Hall, Alabama, take notice of their hometown hero, but the world paid attention and watched with excitement as Wallace overcame exceptional odds on his dynamic journey.

INSPIRATIONAL QUOTES

"I'm an offensive juggernaut. Defense is something I do in my spare time."

"I just go out there and play with all my heart."

"You're supposed to be emotionally connected to the game."

"I'll tell you my legacy: I wasn't welcome. I was too small. I couldn't play the game the way they wanted me to play the game. Sound like an uneven game to me. Put me on a level playing field, and I'll show you."

"Life is what you give it, life is what you take from it. You give life. You take rom life. How much do you take. How much do you leave behind."

TRIVIA QUESTIONS

1. What inspired Ben Wallace to start playing basketball?

A) School program
B) Local basketball team
C) Brother's thrift store-purchased uniforms
D) NBA legend's challenge

2. How did Ben Wallace raise money to attend Charles Oakley's basketball camp?

A) Working at pecan farms
B) Offering haircuts for $3
C) Selling basketball equipment
D) Borrowing from friends

3. What lesson did Ben Wallace learn during a one-on-one game with Charles Oakley?

A) Offensive strategies
B) Defensive techniques
C) Importance of paying attention
D) Basketball fundamentals

4. Which NBA team invited Ben Wallace for a workout prior to the 1996 NBA draft?

A) Boston Celtics
B) New York Knicks
C) Detroit Pistons
D) Los Angeles Lakers

5. What milestone did Ben Wallace achieve in 2021?

A) NBA championship
B) Defensive player of the year
C) Naismith Hall of Fame induction
D) All-American selection

LIFE LESSONS

1. Resilience in the Face of Adversity: Ben Wallace's upbringing in one of the poorest counties in Alabama taught him the importance of resilience. Despite facing economic hardships, he persevered through hard work and determination, proving that challenges can be overcome.

2. Family Bond and Support: The unity within Wallace's family, especially the role of his eldest brother, highlights the significance of family support. Their collective effort to work and support each other played a crucial role in Wallace's journey.

3. Turning Negatives into Positives: Being overlooked by his older siblings on the basketball court didn't discourage Wallace. Instead, he used it as motivation to improve his skills. This lesson emphasizes the power of turning negative situations into opportunities for personal growth.

4. Hard Work and Dedication: Wallace's commitment to improving his game, whether through stealing, rebounding, or saving the ball, underscores the value of hard work and dedication. His work ethic became a key factor in his success both on and off the court.

5. Belief in Oneself: Despite being undrafted and facing skepticism about his abilities, Wallace maintained belief in himself. This lesson teaches the importance of self-confidence and perseverance in the face of doubt, leading to eventual recognition and success.

Trivia Answers

1. C) Brother's thrift store-purchased uniforms
2. B) Offering haircuts for $3
3. C) Importance of paying attention
4. A) Boston Celtics
5. C) Naismith Hall of Fame induction

If you're looking for a great example of how teamwork can make the dream work, look no further than the San Antonio Spurs of the 2000s. Imagine being a five-time NBA champion without a hint of drama in the locker room. That's right, this team actually got along, which helped them become one of the most impressive dynasties in the NBA.

Only a few teams left such a profound mark in the NBA as the Spurs of the 2000s. They marched through a decade with an unparalleled commitment to excellence that would etch the team into the annals of basketball greatness. Let's look deeper at how working together and putting egos aside landed these players in the history books.

Building a great team starts with a solid foundation. The base of the Spurs' dynasty was the dynamic duo of Tim Duncan, known affectionately as "The Big Fundamental," and Coach Gregg Popovich, often referred to as "Pop." Duncan's on-court prowess and Pop's tactical brilliance became the cornerstone of the team's success. Their partnership was synonymous with a commitment to the basics, consistency, and a persistent pursuit of perfection.

Many dynasties build their team around an individual star instead of the team's collective strength. However, the Spurs chose to do the exact opposite. The direction from Pop was clear—prioritize the team over individual accolades. This principle laid the foundation for a dynasty characterized by selflessness, discipline, and an unwavering dedication to a common goal.

The Spurs' reign in the 2000s was marked by a series of triumphs on the grandest stage. They clinched NBA Championships in 1999, 2003, 2005, and 2007, solidifying their status as one of the most dominant teams of the era. Each championship was a testament to their resilience, adaptability, and an uncanny ability to rise to the occasion.

One distinctive feature of the Spurs' dynasty was their embrace of international talent. With players like Manu Ginobili and Tony Parker, the team showcased a global approach to the game. Robert Horry, a veteran and excellent player in the clutch, also joined the team and helped take them to victory. This infusion of diverse styles and perspectives contributed to the Spurs' unique brand of basketball, earning admiration worldwide.

The Spurs were renowned for their exquisite ball movement, a choreography of passes that left opponents struggling to keep up. The emphasis on teamwork was obvious in every play, with players seamlessly passing the ball to find the best shot. No one demanded the ball be passed to them;

the focus was on getting it to the person who was open and could make the shot. This commitment to unselfish basketball became a defining characteristic of the Spurs dynasty.

While offensive brilliance was a hallmark, the Spurs' defensive prowess was equally formidable. Tim Duncan's shot-blocking abilities, coupled with the team's defensive schemes, made them a force to be reckoned with on both ends of the court. The Spurs' commitment to a well-rounded game set them apart in an era marked by specialization.

As we look back on the Spurs dynasty of the 2000s, it's not just the championships that stand out but the lasting legacy of a team that redefined excellence. The commitment to teamwork, the emphasis on fundamentals, and the global influence that they exerted became a blueprint for success that continues to inspire teams across the NBA.

The drama-free atmosphere in their locker room starkly contrasted with the tumultuous situations some of their NBA counterparts faced. In a season where the New York Knicks were marred by public disputes and internal confl cts, the Spurs stood as a beacon of stability. The Knicks, grappling with off-court drama involving Charles Oakley, Derrick Rose's absence on a game night, and Phil Jackson's public criticisms, was a huge difference compared to the focused and drama-free Spurs.

Tim Duncan's personality and success played a pivotal role in shaping the Spurs' culture. Known for his humility, teamwork, and dedication to winning, Duncan set the tone for the entire organization. Players who followed in his footsteps embraced the team-first mentality, turning the Spurs into a model of consistency and professionalism.

RC Buford, alongside Coach Popovich, took on the responsibility of placing the right players around Duncan to ensure championship success. The Spurs' front office, characterized by a unique working relationship between Buford and Popovich, displayed a rare level of cohesion in the ever-evolving landscape of the NBA.

The league underwent significant transformations during the PopBuford era—from isolation-centric playstyles to the rise of super teams and the smallball trend. Despite these changes, the Spurs consistently remained ahead of the curve or adapted swiftly, showcasing their ability to thrive in an evolving basketball landscape.

The Spurs' success wasn't limited to marquee names; their ability to turn overlooked or underperforming players into valuable assets was a testament to their scouting and coaching prowess. Players like Danny Green, Boris Diaw, Patty Mills, and Kawhi Leonard, acquired in a draft night trade for George Hill, flourished under Spurs' system.

Coach Popovich's coaching style, characterized by a no-nonsense yet respectful approach, endeared him to the players. His ability to bring out the best in each individual and consistent principles created an environment conducive to success. Popovich's approach remained unwavering, whether addressing the franchise player or the last man on the bench.

The Spurs dynasty of the 2000s wasn't just a collection of victories but a masterclass in sustained greatness. As we celebrate their achievements, we honor a team that embodied the true spirit of basketball—a symphony of talent, teamwork, and a relentless pursuit of excellence. The legacy of the Spurs dynasty will forever resonate as a shining example of what can be achieved when a team moves in unison toward a shared vision of greatness.

INSPIRATIONAL QUOTES

"We took pride in representing where we came from, took pride in being from small places, and places all around the world and being able to come together and make ourselves into a team, into a group of guys with one goal and get that done." - *Tim Duncan*

"The time when there is no one there to feel sorry for you or to cheer for you is when a player is made." - *Tim Duncan*

"Basketball is a pretty simple game. What wins is consistency and competitiveness." - *Gregg Popovich*

"It's not about any one person. You've got to get over yourself and realize that it takes a group to get this thing done." - *Gregg Popovich*

"The measure of who we are is how we react to something that doesn't go our way." - *Gregg Popovich*

TRIVIA QUESTIONS

1. Who was the dynamic duo at the heart of the San Antonio Spurs' dynasty in the 2000s?

A) Tony Parker and Manu Ginobili
B) Tim Duncan and Gregg Popovich
C) Tim Duncan and Tony Parker
D) Manu Ginobili and Gregg Popovich

2. How many NBA Championships did the Spurs win during their dominant run in the 2000s?

A) 3
B) 4
C) 5
D) 6

3. What was the distinctive feature of the Spurs' playing style that left opponents struggling to keep up?

A) Three-point shooting
B) Isolation plays
C) Exquisite ball movement
D) Aggressive dunks

4. Which player played a pivotal role in shaping the Spurs' culture with his humility, teamwork, and dedication to winning?

A) Manu Ginobili
B) Tony Parker
C) Tim Duncan
D) Gregg Popovich

5. What set the Spurs apart during an era of specialization in playing styles?

A) Offensive brilliance
B) Defensive prowess
C) Superstar players
D) Isolation centric plays

LIFE LESSONS

1. Lesson of Teamwork: The Spurs' dynasty teaches us that building a great team starts with prioritizing collective strength over individual accolades. Working together and putting egos aside can lead to remarkable achievements.

2. Lesson of Resilience: The Spurs' triumphs exemplify resilience, especially in the face of challenges. Life is full of ups and downs, but the ability to adapt, persevere, and rise to the occasion is key to long-term success.

3. Lesson of Leadership: Tim Duncan's leadership style, emphasizing humility and teamwork, showcases the power of leading by example. True leaders create a positive impact in any endeavor by setting the right tone for those around them.

4. Lesson of Adaptability: The Spurs' ability to stay ahead of the curve in the ever-evolving NBA landscape teaches us the importance of adaptability. Embracing change and being flexible are crucial components of sustained success.

5. Lesson of Consistency: The Spurs' consistent success over the years highlights the value of maintaining principles and a no-nonsense yet respectful approach. Being consistent in our values and actions can lead to a lasting legacy of greatness.

Trivia Answers

1. B) Tim Duncan and Gregg Popovich
2. C) 5
3. C) Exquisite ball movement
4. C) Tim Duncan
5. B) Defensive prowess

Can you picture yourself being uprooted and living in another country where you don't speak the language at a very young age? As you struggle to make friends, you're made fun of and ridiculed for looking different, so much of your time is spent alone.

Believe it or not, this was the early childhood experience of one of basketball's greatest prodigies, Kobe Bryant. His adventure began in a faraway land called Italy, where he embarked on a journey filled with challenges, dreams, and the magic of basketball.

At the age of six, Kobe's father, Joe "Jellybean" Bryant, landed a job playing for Sebastiani Rieti, a professional Italian basketball team. The entire family packed their bags and set off to Italy. It was a land of pasta, pizza, and hoop dreams. But in this new place, Kobe faced the challenges of learning a new language and standing out as a young adventurer from a different land.

For young Kobe, living in Italy was like entering a storybook. He had to learn a whole new language, and he even had friends who spoke a different language—Italian!

However, our young hero didn't just learn about basketball during his time in the new land; he also discovered the magic of family bonds and the warmth of new friendships. Yet, amidst the enchantment, there were moments when Kobe faced teasing for his clothes and experienced racism firsthand.

Even in magical places, there are times when people don't understand each other's differences. Fortunately, Kobe always had a love of basketball to motivate him to keep going despite what others thought of him.

Italy became Kobe's playground and the training ground for his exceptional basketball skills. He'd wake up at 6am each morning, ready to go to the gym and practice, practice, practice. It wasn't always easy; sometimes, he played through pain, showing the true meaning of hard work.

As the pages of Kobe's adventure turned, the time came for him to return to the United States at 13 years old. The challenge? Adapting to a place where the language sounded familiar, but the slang and culture were like riddles waiting to be solved. Returning home to the United States felt like stepping into a new chapter. Kobe's Italian clothes and language made him stand out.

Once again, he was the outcast, but he could draw on his experience in Italy and use sports to cultivate relationships with others. He also took the time to develop his game after realizing he was lagging behind the other players. Kobe's competitive spirit could not be quelled.

In an interview with *Fadeaway World*, Kobe recounts, "When I came back to the States, I wasn't the most athletic kid. I couldn't compete with these kids. They're doing windmills and dunking backwards, and I'm happy to tap the back board. So, I had to look at it from a long term, because I wasn't going to give up on the game. So, I had to say 'okay, this year, I'm going to get better at that. Next year, this'. And then so forth and so on. And then patiently I was able to catch them. It's the consistency of the work. Monday, get better. Tuesday, get better. Wednesday, get better. And you do that over a period of time, not 1 month or 2 months. It's 3,4,5,6,7,8,9, 10 years. And then you get to where you want to go."

His drive and tough mentality continued to push Kobe to new heights, and soon, he found himself in the exciting world of the NBA. With a leap of courage, he became the sixth player in history to join the league straight from high school, making history. He went on to become a five-time NBA champion, a two-time NBA Finals MVP, and a two-time Olympic gold medalist.

In a very sad moment in our basketball story, Kobe Bryant, our brave hero, and his daughter Gianna left us on January 26, 2020. They were on a helicopter, heading for a different adventure. The whole world felt deeply sad because Kobe wasn't just a basketball wizard but a friend to many. Even though he's no longer playing on the court, his spirit and the lessons that he shared about working hard, being determined, and caring for our families will always stay with us. Kobe's memory lives on, and we can remember him by playing the game we love with passion and joy, just like he did.

"Every day, it's just constant improvement, constant curiosity, constantly getting better. The results don't really matter. Look at how you deal with the inner challenges, the self-negotiation that takes place inside of our own heads," Kobe's words echo like a guiding light, leaving a lasting impact for generations to come.

INSPIRATIONAL QUOTES

"May you always remember to enjoy the road, especially when it's a hard one."

"If you are going to be a leader, you are not going to please everybody. You have to hold people accountable. Even if you have that moment of being uncomfortable."

"If you're afraid to fail, then you're probably going to fail."

"I have self-doubt. I have insecurity. I have fear of failure. I have nights when I show up at the arena and I'm like, 'My back hurts, my feet hurt, my knees hurt. I don't have it. I just want to chill.' We all have self-doubt. You don't deny it, but you also don't capitulate to it. You embrace it."

"Leadership is lonely, I'm not going to be afraid of confrontation to get us to where we need to go."

TRIVIA QUESTIONS

1. Where did Kobe Bryant spend a significant part of his early childhood?

A) Spain
B) Italy
C) France
D) Germany

2. What motivated Kobe Bryant to wake up at 6am each morning during his time in Italy?

A) Pizza
B) Basketball
C) Learning a new language
D) Playing video games

3. At what age did Kobe Bryant return to the United States?

A) 10
B) 18
C) 16
D) 13

4. What historic milestone did Kobe Bryant achieve in the NBA?

A) Sixth player in history to join the NBA straight from high school
B) First player to score 100 points in a game
C) Most career three-pointers
D) Longest career in NBA history

5. How old was Kobe Bryant when his family moved to Italy?

A) 11
B) 5
C) 6
D) 13

LIFE LESSONS

1. Resilience and Adaptability: Kobe faced the challenge of moving to a foreign country at a young age, where he didn't speak the language. Despite being ridiculed and facing cultural differences, he adapted, learned a new language, and thrived.

2. Family Bonds and Friendship: Kobe discovered the magic of family bonds and the warmth of new friendships during his time in Italy. These relationships became essential sources of support and motivation throughout his life.

3. Overcoming Adversity with Passion: Despite experiencing teasing and racism, Kobe's love for basketball motivated him to persevere. He used the sport as a tool to overcome challenges and stay focused on his goals.

4. Consistency and Long-Term Vision: Kobe emphasized the importance of consistency and having a long-term vision. His dedication to improving every day, over many years, allowed him to catch up and eventually excel in basketball.

5. Inner Challenges and Self-Negotiation: Kobe highlighted the significance of dealing with inner challenges and self-negotiation. He encouraged constant improvement, curiosity, and the ability to overcome obstacles within one's own mind.

Trivia Answers

1. B) Italy
2. B) Basketball
3. D) 13
4. A) Sixth player in history to join the NBA straight from high school
5. C) 6

Whenever the Chicago Bulls of the 1990s are mentioned, most automatically think of superstar Michael Jordan. Others fondly remember the duo of Jordan and Scottie Pippen controlling the court. But the truth is that others made significant contributions to the Bulls' successful reign in the 1990s.

Dennis Rodman was considered a rebel, a player who was hard to control on and off the court. There were also other big personalities like Horace Grant and important role players, including Bill Cartwright, John Paxson, B.J. Armstrong, Will Perdue, and Steve Kerr, to name a few. However, managing all these personalities and ensuring winning seasons was left up to one man—Phil Jackson.

Jackson, often referred to as the "Zen Master" of basketball coaching, was crucial in bringing the team together. He believed in the power of teamwork and encouraged players to be selfless for the team's greater good. Each team member has the same goal—to win—and Jackson pushed everyone to keep the larger goal in mind.

Creating a unified team wasn't without its challenges. For instance, there was a time when Pippen and Rodman needed Jackson to mediate a conflict. Rodman had injured Pippen in the past during a game, but to join the Bulls, Jackson asked Rodman to apologize. Rodman was reluctant at first but eventually understood the importance of building strong relationships within the team and put his ego aside to apologize.

Jackson's coaching style was unique. He believed in openness, communication, and dialogue, even when facing internal conflicts. When a book revealed tension within the team, Jackson saw it as an opportunity to strengthen cohesion rather than avoid the issues. He applied the "Plus Principle," where honest feedback and constructive criticism were essential for effective teamwork.

Phil Jackson transformed conflicts into opportunities for growth and learning. He practiced "depersonalized criticism," focusing on improving performance rather than attacking individuals. Jackson created a framework where critiques were seen as chances to enhance the team's overall performance.

Inspired by Native American wisdom, Jackson implemented a multifaceted program to strengthen team cohesion. He emphasized the importance of being responsible to the team and working together toward a common goal.

Despite the fragility of team bonds, Jackson's dedication paid off, turning the Bulls into a six-time championship-winning team in the 1990s. Ultimately, anyone who played under Jackson learned that communication and respect go a long way when laying the foundations for strong, lasting relationships

Although it sounds like a fairytale, the journey to winning those six championships was filled with ups and downs. Let's take a quick look at how it all unfolded, starting at the beginning.

The 1989-90 season is when the groundwork for the Bulls dynasty was laid. That was the season that Michael Jordan, Scottie Pippen, and Horace Grant formed a trio that would define an era.

Throughout their journey, one of the challenges that tested the Bulls dominance was Scottie Pippen's famous migraine headache in the 1990 Eastern Conference finals. It could have been a stumbling block, but instead, it fueled the team's resolve. After a disheartening loss to the Pistons in Game 7, Michael Jordan's unwavering determination and leadership propelled the Bulls to vow never to experience such a heartbreaking loss again.

Their mental toughness on the court propelled the Bulls to their first NBA championship in 1991. Jordan's exceptional talent and undeniable leadership earned him the Finals MVP title. That was the watershed moment that marked the beginning of a journey that would land them in the history books.

Building on their initial success, the Bulls continued to rewrite the record books. The 1991-92 season saw them secure a league-best 67-15 record, leading to their second NBA title after sweeping the Portland Trail Blazers in the Finals. Jordan's prowess was once again on display as he was once again named the Finals MVP. In 1993, the Bulls clinched their third championship in six games against the Phoenix Suns, solidifying their status as a basketball powerhouse.

Following the third consecutive championship, Michael Jordan stunned the basketball world by briefly retiring from the sport to pursue a baseball career. His absence left a void in the league, and provided a chance for other players and teams to flourish. One of those new contenders were the Houston Rockets. However, the chance for other teams to showcase their skills in the NBA finals was short-lived with the return of Jordan in 1995.

The 1995-96 season was a historic chapter for the Bulls as they achieved a league-best 72-10 record, surpassing all expectations. Jordan, once again the Finals MVP, led the team to a sweep against the Seattle SuperSonics.

Unstoppable, the Bulls continued their triumphant march in the 1996-97 season, securing their fifth championship by defeating the Utah Jazz in six games. Jordan's game-winner in Game 6 and his fifth MVP award added another layer to his legendary status. The crowning moment came in 1998, with the Bulls capturing their sixth and final championship against the Utah Jazz. Jordan's 45-point performance in Game 6 and his sixth Finals MVP award marked the culmination of an extraordinary era.

The 1997-98 season, aptly dubbed "The Last Dance" by coach Phil Jackson, was a culmination of a dynasty. Despite internal challenges and uncertainties about the team's future, the Bulls showcased their championship mentality. Jordan's iconic pose with the championship trophy after Game 6 of the Finals marked the end of an era.

The Bulls' reign may have ended in 1998, but their legacy lives on. Michael Jordan's remarkable talent and leadership, coupled with the team's collective efforts, resulted in six championships in eight years—an unprecedented achievement. The Bulls' journey symbolizes basketball excellence and is a testament to teamwork, resilience, and leadership.

As we reflect on the 1990s Chicago Bulls, we recognize a team that transcended the confines of the court. Their accomplishments continue to inspire basketball enthusiasts worldwide, reminding us of an era where greatness was achieved and sustained. The 1990s Chicago Bulls is a team that etched its name in history books and left an enduring legacy that will be remembered for generations to come.

INSPIRATIONAL QUOTES

"The strength of the team is each individual member. The strength of each member is the team." - Phil Jackson

"The sign of a great player is how much he elevates his colleagues' performance." - Phil Jackson

"Basketball is a great mystery. You can do everything right. You can have the perfect mix of talent and the best system of offense in the game. You can devise a foolproof defensive strategy and prepare your players for every possible eventuality. But if the players don't have a sense of oneness as a group, your efforts won't pay off. And the bond that unites a team can be so fragile, so elusive." - Phil Jackson

"I can accept failure, everyone fails at something. But I can't accept not trying." - Michael Jordan

"Basketball is a lifelong game. You continue to learn from the game day in and day out, and all along the way, you get better" - Scottie Pippen

TRIVIA QUESTIONS

1. Who was known as the "Zen Master" of basketball coaching for the 1990s Chicago Bulls?

A) Michael Jordan
B) Scottie Pippen
C) Dennis Rodman
D) Phil Jackson

2. What conflict did Phil Jackson mediate between two key players in the Bulls, Pippen and Rodman?

A) Injury during a game
B) Argument about team strategy
C) Personal dispute from off-court incidents
D) Competitive rivalry in practice

3. Besides Michael Jordan and Scottie Pippen, who are mentioned as significant contributors to the Bulls' success?

A) Bill Cartwright
B) John Paxson
C) B.J. Armstrong
D) All of the above

4. What coaching principle did Phil Jackson apply to strengthen team cohesion, involving honest feedback and constructive criticism?

A) Team-First Approach
B) Plus Principle
C) Individual Excellence Rule
D) Unity Strategy

5. How did Phil Jackson view conflicts within the team?

A) Avoid them at all costs
B) Embrace them for personal growth
C) Turn them into opportunities for learning
D) Use them to identify weak links in the team

LIFE LESSONS

1. The Power of Teamwork: Despite individual talents, the Chicago Bulls' success in the 1990s was built on the power of teamwork and selflessness. How can you apply this lesson in your own collaborative efforts?

2. Conflict Resolution: The story of Pippen and Rodman highlights the importance of effective conflict resolution. Sometimes, putting aside personal differences for the greater goal can lead to stronger relationships. How do you handle conflicts within your team or relationships?

3. Openness and Communication: Phil Jackson's coaching style emphasized openness, communication, and dialogue, even during challenging times. How can fostering open communication contribute to the success of a team or group?

4. Constructive Criticism: The "Plus Principle" encourages honest feedback and constructive criticism for effective teamwork. How can you implement depersonalized criticism to enhance your performance or your team?

5. Building Lasting Relationships: The story suggests that communication and respect are essential for laying the foundations for strong and lasting relationships. How can you incorporate these elements into your interactions to foster strong bonds and unity?

Trivia Answers

1. D) Phil Jackson
2. A) Injury during a game
3. D) All of the above
4. B) Plus Principle
5. C) Turn them into opportunities for learning

Unlock an even deeper appreciation for basketball with our exclusive free content: "100 Unique General Facts and Trivia Questions on Basketball." This resource is meticulously curated to enhance your understanding and enjoyment of the game. Whether you're a budding enthusiast or a seasoned fan, these facts and trivia questions will expand your knowledge, challenge your understanding, and provide hours of fun. Discover intriguing details about the sport's history, iconic players, and memorable moments that have shaped basketball as we know it today. To access this invaluable resource, simply scan the QR code provided and start your journey into the fascinating world of basketball trivia and facts.

Once upon a time, a remarkable girl named Diana Taurasi had a unique journey to becoming a basketball star. Her mother, with roots in Argentina, and her father, a native of Italy, made their way to the United States, settling in Los Angeles. As a little family, they later moved to Chino, California, where Diana felt a strong connection that this was her home.

Being the daughter of immigrants filled her with pride and shaped her upbringing. In her house, they spoke Spanish, listened to Spanish music, and watched TV channels in Spanish. Their meals were a delightful mix of Italian and Argentinian flavors.

In an interview with Sports Illustrated (SI), she remembered a funny moment at a friend's house, where they had spaghetti with meat sauce and a glass of milk. Milk was not the drink she had expected. Still, it helped her realize that America was full of unique cultures and combinations.

At 13, her family spent a year back in Argentina, and she had a chance to experience the struggles that her extended family experienced. This added a unique layer to her identity and fueled a determination not to waste any opportunities when they returned to California.

Her parents worked tirelessly to build a better life. Her dad's early morning commute and her mom's odd jobs were all part of creating something special for their family. This duality, the insider's feeling of opportunity, and the outsider's understanding of privilege became a part of her.

Taurasi also embraced duality in her love for two sports—soccer from her Argentine roots and basketball, the quintessential American playground game. Her parents encouraged her to pursue both, and she cherished memories of playing in the driveway, waiting for her dad to get home, and transitioning from the soccer field to the basketball court.

Although she liked soccer more, her dad, foreseeing opportunities in basketball, encouraged her to play basketball. This decision led to her playing organized basketball in sixth grade, receiving recruitment letters, and eventually being noticed by UConn's Geno Auriemma.

The transition to college at UConn wasn't easy, and many of her teammates found her annoying. It was fairly early in the season when Taurasi decided to hold an impromptu concert on a bus ride and serenade everyone with her version of OutKast's "Ms. Jackson." Unfortunately for Taurasi, her teammates did not like her rendition. Taurasi soon found herself locked in the bathroom in the back of the bus for the remainder of the ride.

Acclimating to the team was a struggle, but she

embraced the challenge, and stepped up her play on the court. Taurasi became a force to be reckoned with on the basketball court, and although her team lost the championship in her freshman year, she made sure they never lost in the NCAA tournament again.

Moving on to the professional level in the WNBA was a new challenge. Drafted first overall by the Phoenix Mercury, Taurasi faced the demands and expectations of a whole new world. Now, she was playing with grown women who were stronger and smarter. To overcome this obstacle, she focused on getting better each day.

Taurasi needed to adjust to Coach Westhead's run-and-gun, high-octane offense. Implementing it during Taurasi's first season took time, but it took the team just missing the playoffs for her to finally understand "The System." The next season found the Mercury winning their first WNBA championship with Taurasi at the helm.

Her basketball journey took her overseas to Russia during off seasons, presenting new challenges, but she chose to engage with the unknown, taking the path less traveled.

Taurasi's willingness to embrace change and challenge herself has won her a few accolades, including three WNBA championships and five Olympic gold medals. Her story shows that embracing challenges, engaging with the unknown, and being true to oneself can lead you to an epic adventure, just like the kid from Chino who became a basketball star.

INSPIRATIONAL QUOTES

"My sense of home, and where I'm from, has helped to shape but also ground me. No matter how far across the map my basketball journey has taken me or how bright the lights, I'm still myself."

"Success is not final, failure is not fatal: It is the courage to continue that counts."

"You have to believe in yourself when no one else does - that makes you a winner right there."

"The only limit to our realization of tomorrow will be our doubts of today."

"Hard work beats talent when talent doesn't work hard."

TRIVIA QUESTIONS

1. What was Diana Taurasi's initial preference in sports during her childhood?

A) Soccer
B) Basketball
C) Tennis
D) Swimming

2. During her family's year in Argentina, what did Diana Taurasi gain from the experience?

A) Increased knowledge of Italian culture
B) Understanding of her extended family's struggles
C) Improved proficiency in the Spanish language
D) Exposure to diverse American cultures

3. Where did Diana Taurasi play organized basketball for the first time?

A) Argentina
B) Los Angeles
C) Chino, California
D) UConn

4. Which WNBA team drafted Diana Taurasi first overall?

A) Los Angeles Sparks
B) Seattle Storm
C) Connecticut Sun
D) Phoenix Mercury

5. How did Diana Taurasi overcome the challenges of playing in the WNBA with grown women?

A) By avoiding off-season play
B) By focusing on getting better each day
C) By quitting basketball and pursuing soccer
D) By seeking support from her parents

LIFE LESSONS

1. **Embrace Cultural Diversity:** Diana Taurasi's upbringing, influenced by her parents' roots in Argentina and Italy, highlights the value of embracing and celebrating cultural diversity. This exposure to different cultures enriched her life and worldview.

2. **Work Ethic and Perseverance:** Taurasi's parents worked tirelessly to build a better life for their family. Her dad's early morning commute and her mom's odd jobs exemplify the importance of a strong work ethic and perseverance in overcoming challenges.

3. **Duality and Adaptability:** Taurasi embraced duality in her love for both soccer and basketball. Her ability to adapt and transition between different aspects of her identity and interests reflects the importance of being adaptable and open to change.

4. **Seizing Opportunities:** Taurasi's determination not to waste any opportunities, especially after experiencing the struggles of her extended family in Argentina, underscores the importance of seizing opportunities and making the most out of them.

5. **Courage to Take the Path Less Traveled:** Taurasi's willingness to engage with the unknown, such as playing basketball overseas in Russia during off seasons, demonstrates the courage to take the path less traveled. This life lesson encourages individuals to embrace challenges and explore new territories.

Trivia Answers

1. A) Soccer
2. B) Understanding of her extended family's struggles
3. C) Chino, California
4. D) Phoenix Mercury
5. B) By focusing on getting better each day

Basketball is undoubtedly a big man's game. The average height of an NBA player is 6 feet 6 inches, and even the guys that are considered small, the point guards, are 6 feet 2 inches on average. That is still taller than the average man in the United States, who is typically 5 feet 9 inches. So, what happens when you're shorter than average but have dreams of being one of the NBA's best? All you have to do is look to the story of Earl Boykins who at 5 feet 5 inches ignored his doubters and became a basketball phenomenon.

It was obvious early in Boykins' life that he wouldn't likely grow to be six feet tall with his mother Charlene standing at only 4 feet 11 inches, and his father, Willie, at 5 feet 8 inches. But that wouldn't deter him from pursuing his dream. Boykins' deep connection to basketball began when he was just a three-year-old toddler being snuck into gyms in his father's duffle bag. Willie had a reverent love for basketball and played in small night leagues across his city of Cleveland, Ohio. Soon, Boykins would find himself on the court competing in leisure leagues. It was a sight to see as this small boy ran up and down the court, hustling right along with his father and other adult teammates.

Boykins was able to keep up with the grown men due to his father's persistent cross-fit training which began in fifth grade and lasted until he was a senior in high school. As the young Boykins navigated the landscape of high school hoops, Cleveland Central Catholic bore witness to his ascent. Averaging an astounding 24.6 points per game, he led his team to a remarkable 23–2 record, earning the distinction of being the best high school basketball player in the Cleveland area during the 1990s.

He used his size to his advantage in developing his game. Boykins' low-to-the-ground ball-handling skills and lightning quickness kept defenders on their toes. He also had a killer jump shot that he could finish from just about anywhere on the court. The man was a star in Cleveland; however, the accolades and praise he received in his hometown were tempered by the lack of Division I scholarship offers, with only Eastern Michigan and Iowa extending opportunities, the latter of which later withdrew.

Although Boykins' father's tough physical training was a source of strain in their relationship, once Boykins reached Eastern Michigan, he appreciated what his father had done. Willie understood what it would take for someone of Earl's height to succeed on a professional level and made sure he instilled it in his son. Boykins' saw that he was miles ahead of his teammates at Eastern Michigan when it came to conditioning, and with the help of his dad's coaching, Boykins became the team's starting point guard.

Undeterred by the perceived limitations, Earl embraced the challenges of college basketball at Eastern Michigan University. The MAC tournaments of 1996 and 1998 became the stages where he showcased his mettle, leading his team to victory. All-Mid-American Conference first-team honors in his junior and senior years and a second-place finish in NCAA Men's Division I Basketball Championship scoring charts solidified his legacy.

But, once again, Boykins' accolades and consistency would be largely ignored by NBA teams. The draft came and went without anyone picking up Boykins. Still, Boykins' tenacity was able to draw the attention of a few and short-term contracts paved the way for a groundbreaking five-year, $13.7 million deal with the Denver Nuggets, marking the beginning of a historic chapter. He'd finally made it, and on November 11, 2004, Earl etched his name in the record books as the shortest player to score 30 or more points in an NBA game.

A journeyman's odyssey ensued, weaving through the rosters of various NBA teams and even crossing international borders to Italy's Virtus Bologna. The Washington Wizards welcomed Boykins as he made a triumphant return to the NBA, playing a pivotal role after guards Gilbert Arenas and Javaris Crittenton's suspension. His one-year deal with the Milwaukee Bucks in 2010 and a 10-day contract with the Houston Rockets in 2012 punctuated the last stages of his NBA career.

If you think Boykins was finished with basketball, though, you're wrong. The summer of 2017 witnessed his participation in The Basketball Tournament, where he led his team to two victories with an average of 24.5 points per game. Fan letters poured in, attesting to his impact as parents thanked him for inspiring their undersized children.

Earl Boykins, the second-shortest player in NBA history, transcended the boundaries of physical stature to become a symbol of tenacity and inspiration. He shows us why we shouldn't listen to detractors who only tell us what we can't do. Boykins was ridiculed for his height but took it in stride and responded in court, proving the naysayers wrong.

His mantra echoes through the courts of life: "I don't look at my height as a disadvantage; I'm unique." Boykins certainly is unique and had a 13-year run in the NBA, something many big men desire but don't attain. In that time, he was able to score 5,791 career points and 2,092 assists in a league of giants.

Earl Boykins stood tall, proving that with unwavering determination, even the smallest can achieve the extraordinary. His legacy continues to inspire generations, a testament to the indomitable spirit of a true basketball hero.

INSPIRATIONAL QUOTES

"The scoring will come. The most important part of the playoffs is your defense. We are playing well on defense. You win games on defense."

"There are no days off for me. I have to work longer and harder than everyone else to be successful."

"I'm improving every day, gaining more strength in my hand, more flexibility."

"You don't have to shoot great to still get the victory. As long as you do all the other things on the court, you can be OK."

"Whenever you lose, you're concerned. But we've got to stay confident."

TRIVIA QUESTIONS

1. What is Earl Boykins' height, making him the second-shortest player in NBA history?

A) 5 feet 2 inches
B) 5 feet 5 inches
C) 6 feet 0 inches
D) 5 feet 9 inches

2. In which city did Earl Boykins play high school basketball, leading his team to a remarkable 23–2 record?

A) Cleveland, Ohio
B) Los Angeles, California
C) Chicago, Illinois
D) New York City, New York

3. What significant achievement did Earl Boykins reach on November 11, 2004, in an NBA game?

A) Scored 20 three-pointers
B) Recorded a triple-double
C) Became the shortest player to score 30 or more points
D) Dunked over a 7-foot opponent

4. During his NBA career, which team marked a triumphant return for Earl Boykins after the suspension of guards Gilbert Arenas and Javaris Crittenton?

A) Denver Nuggets
B) Washington Wizards
C) Milwaukee Bucks
D) Houston Rockets

5. In the summer of 2017, Earl Boykins participated in which basketball tournament, leading his team to two victories?

A) NBA Finals
B) March Madness
C) The Basketball Tournament
D) EuroLeague

LIFE LESSONS

1. Resilience in the Face of Doubt: Earl Boykins faced skepticism due to his height, typically considered a disadvantage in basketball. However, he remained resilient and determined to pursue his dream despite the doubts of others. The lesson here is to stay committed to your goals, even when faced with skepticism or challenges.

2. Hard Work and Discipline Pay Off: Boykins' success wasn't solely based on his natural talent; his father's persistent cross-fit training played a crucial role. The consistent training from a young age helped him develop skills that set him apart. This underscores the importance of hard work, discipline, and continuous improvement in achieving success.

3. Adaptability and Skill Development: Boykins used his smaller stature to his advantage by developing unique skills, such as low-to-the-ground ball handling and lightning-quick moves. The lesson is to adapt to your circumstances and focus on developing skills that make you stand out, turning potential limitations into strengths.

4. Overcoming Setbacks: Despite facing setbacks like limited scholarship offers and going undrafted in the NBA, Boykins didn't let these obstacles define his journey. He adapted, persevered, and eventually secured a significant NBA contract. The lesson is to view setbacks as growth opportunities and keep pushing forward despite initial challenges.

5. Embrace Uniqueness and Self-Confidence: Boykins embraced his uniqueness, viewing his height not as a disadvantage but as something that made him stand out. His self-confidence and acceptance of his uniqueness allowed him to excel on the court. The lesson here is to embrace your individuality, believe in yourself, and use your unique qualities to your advantage.

Trivia Answers

1. B) 5 feet 5 inches
2. A) Cleveland, Ohio
3. C) Became the shortest player to score 30 or more points
4. B) Washington Wizards
5. C) The Basketball Tournament

Professional sports teams are typically found in large metropolitan areas. That's because these regions have substantial populations, which is great for putting fans in seats. Then there's the local marketing and sponsorship opportunities which are abundant. These factors matter when trying to recruit and keep top talent on the roster.

The team doesn't just take from the surrounding community, it also gives back in a few ways. Not only do franchises generate jobs, they also stimulate the local economy as bars and restaurants benefit from patrons going out to catch the game near the stadium. Even eateries that aren't near the arena see a lift in business when fans throw watch parties at the establishments.

There's a civic pride that grows among the local residents and a sense of community as everyone joins together to support the home team. But happens when a team exists in a small market?

Many sports analysts don't believe a major team can thrive or have a significant impact on the community if it isn't in a large market, and in many cases they are not wrong. However, there is one team that defies this notion: the Connecticut Sun.

It all began with the UConn Huskies winning their first NCAA title in 1995, just the first of 10 championships they'd go on to win. The Gampel Pavilion rocked with booming cheers during sold out nights, and the love for the sport spread throughout the tiny state. Connecticut showed a profound passion for women's basketball.

Then, something completely unexpected happened. Inspired by basketball fervor sweeping the state, the Mohegan Tribe bought a major-league professional franchise. The WNBA's Orlando Miracle was acquired by the tribe in 2002, bringing the team to their resort casino in rural Eastern Connecticut. However, this location was far from bustling urban centers.

The team, known as the Sun, faced a unique challenge. Playing in a small market, away from major airports and the visibility of big cities, they stood at a crossroads. In a league where players sought endorsement opportunities and visibility in metropolitan markets like New York and Los Angeles, where did the quiet rural town of Uncasville, fit in the evolving WNBA?

Finding their place wouldn't be easy as the Sun were living in the shadow of a college giant. Then, there was also the professional team that came before them and folded, the ABL's new England Blizzard. There was a hole left in the hearts of women's basketball fans that needed to be filled. In 2002, a glimmer of hope was restored as the Mohegan Sun Casino considered purchasing a WNBA team.

Mitchell Etess, the Sun's visionary, persistently pursued the idea despite initial reservations from the NBA. He saw the potential of being the first Native American tribe to own a major league sports franchise and embraced the opportunity to bring professional women's basketball to the heart of Connecticut.

The journey to bring the Sun to Connecticut was challenging because there was some hesitancy to sell a team to a casino. Some felt that associating with a casino would open the team up to backlash from those who believe that gambling is wrong.

Still, with determination, negotiations, and a bit of uncertainty, the tribe purchased the Orlando Miracle, rebranded it as the Connecticut Sun, and moved it to Uncasville in January 2003. Professional sports made a triumphant return to the state, bringing joy to fans six years after the NHL Whalers left Hartford.

The Sun found its head coach in Mike Thibault, and despite the delay in the 2003 season due to labor strife, Thibault, Etess, and the team had the time to prepare. From ordering uniforms to creating a mascot, they embraced every challenge.

The introduction season of 2003 saw the Sun shining bright, even though they fell to the reigning champions. With a season record of 18-16, the new team made it to the Eastern Conference Finals, capturing the hearts of fans.

The years rolled by and the WNBA's growth soared to new heights, both on and off the court. The courts were filled with dazzling talent, drawing more viewers than ever. With this surge in popularity, players found unprecedented opportunities to build their brands and earn recognition beyond the basketball arena.

Amidst this flourishing era, talk of expansion buzzed in the air. Now more player-driven than ever, the league eyed potential markets like the Bay Area, Toronto, Denver, and Charlotte. However, amidst the excitement, a challenge loomed for smaller markets like Connecticut.

Some players, like Lindsay Whalen, became household names, the team's location posed hurdles in signing the league's biggest stars. The proximity to major cities was limited, and the absence of flashy lights left the Sun in a different league.

Coach Thibault acknowledged the struggle in attracting top players. The team built its roster through the draft or trades, lacking the allure that captures the attention of seasoned vets and rookies looking to make a name for themselves. The nearest airport was an hour away and had limited direct flights, making travel a bit of an inconvenience.

Instead of viewing these challenges as a negative, Sun President Rizzotti decided to lean in and spin them as positives. She highlighted the benefits of avoiding city traffic and emphasized the convenience of travel logistics. The Sun, she believed, could only benefit from future developments like charter flights, making their journey even smoother.

To counteract the limitations of their market size, the Sun embraced a "must-win" attitude on the court and prioritized treating players as individuals off the court. Sienko emphasized the Mohegan Sun way, ensuring players experienced the best amenities and were personally and professionally cared for.

Still, some players sought opportunities in larger markets. Both former Sun stars Tina Charles and Jonquel Jones left for bigger cities, citing the desire for championship victories and broader brand-building opportunities. Building individual brands in a state already captivated by UConn posed an additional challenge. However, the Sun's success on the court and a loyal fan base spoke volumes.

Connecticut's small market success became evident as the Sun ranked third in the league and boasted an average attendance of 6,392 fans. Thibault reflected on the team's unique position, being the first individually owned, non-NBA-owned team in a casino in a small market. Against all odds, they made it work and set a standard that many once questioned.

As the Sun basked in success, becoming the first WNBA team to turn a profit in just seven years, they became an anchor for the league and a source of inspiration for fans building loyalty to the Sun. And the Sun showing appreciation for that loyalty established the Connecticut Sun Foundation in 2007.

The foundation regularly donates to local nonprofits like "Steals for Meals," a program dedicated to fighting family food insecurity. Another organization that the Sun gives back to includes The Village for Families and Children, a group that supports mental healthcare. Then there's "Threes for Degrees," the Sun's scholarship program that donates $100 for every three-pointer made by a Sun's player during the season's home games.

The radiant move to Connecticut not only brought professional women's basketball to the state but also a philanthropic philosophy that consistently supports the community. The Sun use their bountiful resources to ensure their local supporters know how much they're appreciated. And so, the Sun continues to rise, illuminating the world of women's basketball in Connecticut and around the globe.

INSPIRATIONAL QUOTES

"It's another sport mentally, where you have to go to another level when it comes to mental toughness and just toughness in general." - Alyssa Thomas, Forward

"Let your smile change the world. Never let the world change your smile." - Brionna Thomas, Forward

"Whenever time get hard, or the teasing gets rough... Accept yourself first, every day and every season because God made you this way for a reason." - Dewanna Bonner, Guard

"No matter what anyone else want you to be or think, there's more than enough space so you never have to shrink." - Dewanna Bonner

"Always remember that you are awesome and amazing, resilient and tough - but most of all, you are more than enough." - Dewanna Bonner

TRIVIA QUESTIONS

1. What inspired the Mohegan Tribe to buy a WNBA team and bring it to Connecticut?

A) Soccer Fever
B) Basketball Fever
C) Baseball Craze
D) Golf Enthusiasm

2. In which year did the Mohegan Tribe purchase the WNBA's Orlando Miracle and relocate it to Connecticut?

A) 1995
B) 2002
C) 2007
D) 2010

3. How did the Sun's leadership view the challenges of their small market size?

A) Negatively, as insurmountable obstacles
B) Positively, as opportunities for growth
C) Indifferently, without taking any specific stance
D) Ambivalently, with mixed feelings

4. What philanthropic program supports family food insecurity, initiated by the Connecticut Sun Foundation?

A) Dunks for Drinks
B) Slams for Snacks
C) Steals for Meals
D) Blocks for Bites

5. Which former Sun stars left for bigger cities, citing the desire for championship victories and broader brand-building opportunities?

A) Diana Taurasi and Sue Bird
B) Tamika Catchings and Maya Moore
C) Tina Charles and Jonquel Jones
D) Skylar Diggins-Smith and Elena Delle Donne

LIFE LESSONS

1. Overcoming Challenges and Defying Expectations: The Connecticut Sun faced unique challenges, being in a small market away from major cities. Despite initial doubts and hesitancy, the team overcame obstacles related to location, market size, and perceptions associated with owning a team in a casino. The lesson here is to persevere and pursue your goals even when faced with unconventional or unexpected challenges.

2. Innovation and Adaptability: The Sun demonstrated innovation and adaptability in creating a successful WNBA team in an unconventional setting. Mitchell Etess's persistence, the tribe's vision, and the team's ability to adapt to challenges such as player recruitment showcased the importance of being flexible and open to unconventional solutions in achieving success.

3. Building Community and Civic Pride: The team's presence in a small market fostered a strong sense of community and civic pride among local residents. The lesson is the impact of sports teams on bringing people together, fostering a shared identity, and contributing to the local community's well-being. It emphasizes the role of sports in building connections beyond just entertainment.

4. Turning Challenges into Strengths: Instead of viewing the limitations of their market size as negatives, the Sun leadership embraced them as positives. The emphasis on avoiding city traffic, highlighting travel logistics, and creating a unique team culture showed the power of reframing challenges and turning them into strengths. This lesson encourages finding opportunities within constraints.

5. Philanthropy and Giving Back: The establishment of the Connecticut Sun Foundation and the team's commitment to philanthropy showcase the importance of giving back to the community. Through programs like "Steals for Meals," supporting mental healthcare, and providing scholarships, the Sun demonstrated the impact sports organizations can have in addressing societal issues and making a positive difference.

Trivia Answers

1. B) Basketball Fever
2. B) 2002
3. B) Positively, as opportunities for growth

4. C) Steals for Meals
5. C) Tina Charles and Jonquel Jones

When talking about NBA dynasties, a few teams immediately come to mind. Names like the Boston Celtics, Los Angeles Lakers, and Chicago Bulls are just a few legendary teams that have won several Finals competitions.

But these guys aren't the only ones who can snatch multiple championship titles. It's time to recognize the WNBAs Minnesota Lynx and add them to the conversation. From 2011 to 2017, this group of remarkable women forged a path to greatness, leaving an indelible mark on the history of the WNBA.

The Lynx's incredible journey began in 2011, a year that marked a turning point for the franchise. After a rough 2010 season, where they finished 13-21, the team underwent a remarkable transformation.

With head coach Cheryl Reeve leading the charge in her second year and fueled by a talented roster, the Lynx secured their first title in franchise history. She was the mastermind behind the 180-degree turn the team made and helped shape them as a basketball powerhouse.

What made these years truly special was the extraordinary group of players who formed the backbone of this championship era. These athletes, bound by a common goal, will forever be celebrated as legends in the Lynx's history. Let's take a closer look at the women who helped take the team to numerous victories.

A beacon of inspiration, Maya Moore's dazzling skills and leadership earned her the WNBA MVP in 2014. With four league titles and a Finals MVP in 2013, Moore's legacy is etched in Lynx history.

Seimone Augustus, with her eight All-Star appearances and six All-WNBA picks, embodied a winning spirit. After returning from a challenging injury, she played a pivotal role in the 2011 Finals. Her historic performance, averaging 22.0 points per game, showcased resilience and determination, earning her the Finals MVP title. The defining moment set the stage for the Lynx's dominance.

Hailing from Minnesota, Lindsay Whalen not only entered the Naismith Hall of Fame in 2022, but also became the team's all-time assists leader. Her four league championships and two Olympic gold medals are a testament to her enduring legacy.

In 2015, the Lynx orchestrated a masterful move by acquiring Sylvia Fowles, the best center in WNBA history. A force on both ends of the court, Fowles, the league MVP in 2017, secured two WNBA championships. With numerous accolades, including two Finals MVP awards, she redefined excellence in the paint.

Defensive powerhouse Rebekkah Brunson's five All-WNBA defensive team selections and four league championships make her an integral part of the Lynx's triumphs.

Unforgettable moments punctuated the Lynx's road to success. There was the visionary pass from Janel McCarville to Rebekkah Brunson in the 2013 Finals that exemplified the teamwork it takes to be a champion. Then there's Maya Moore's game-winning three with 1.7 seconds left on the clock in the 2015 Finals.

In the thrilling world of the WNBA, the Minnesota Lynx stand tall as the true champions of the 2010s. With four titles under their belt, they emerged as the dynasty of the decade, leaving a legacy that will inspire generations to come.

INSPIRATIONAL QUOTES

"You have to be able to bounce back and deal with disappointment, failure and weaknesses, and a lot of that happens behind the scenes for teams that are very successful." - Maya Moore, former Forward

"Stop making excuses and start making your free throws." - Maya Moore

"My dad taught me that you have to work hard for anything you want in life, and I wanted to be good at playing basketball." - Seimone Augustus, former Guard

"... it's all about the team. If you get too caught up in your own individual awards, it takes away from your focus and it takes away from being part of the team. Always put the team first." - Lindsay Whalen, former Point Guard

"You earn victories like this just by sticking with it and digging down." - Lindsay Whalen

TRIVIA QUESTIONS

1. Who was the head coach of the Minnesota Lynx during their championship era from 2011 to 2017?

A) Cheryl Reeve
B) Maya Moore
C) Seimone Augustus
D) Lindsay Whalen

2. In which year did the Lynx secure their first WNBA title in franchise history?

A) 2011
B) 2013
C) 2015
D) 2017

3. Which player earned the WNBA MVP in 2014 and is considered a beacon of inspiration for the Lynx?

A) Seimone Augustus
B) Maya Moore
C) Lindsay Whalen
D) Sylvia Fowles

4. Who played a pivotal role in the 2011 Finals for the Lynx, showcasing resilience and determination after overcoming a challenging injury?

A) Maya Moore
B) Seimone Augustus
C) Lindsay Whalen
D) Rebekkah Brunson

5. In 2015, the Lynx acquired Sylvia Fowles, considered the best center in WNBA history. In which year did Fowles secure the league MVP award?

A) 2011
B) 2013
C) 2015
D) 2017

LIFE LESSONS

1. Resilience and Transformation: The Lynx's remarkable transformation from a challenging season in 2010 to winning multiple championships underscores the importance of resilience. Life is filled with ups and downs, but the ability to bounce back and undergo positive transformations is key to long-term success.

2. Teamwork and Collaboration: The unforgettable moments, like the visionary pass in the 2013 Finals, highlight the significance of teamwork. Success often requires collaboration and a shared goal. Recognizing and valuing the strengths of each team member can lead to achieving greatness together.

3. Overcoming Adversity: Seimone Augustus's comeback from a challenging injury in 2011 demonstrates the power of perseverance and determination. Life is bound to present challenges, but facing them head-on and pushing through can lead to personal growth and success.

4. Leadership and Legacy: The leadership of figures like Maya Moore and the coaching prowess of Cheryl Reeve showcases the impact of effective leadership. Building a legacy involves personal achievements and positively influencing and inspiring others. Leaders can leave a lasting mark on the people and organizations they lead.

5. Continuous Improvement: The Lynx's strategic move in acquiring Sylvia Fowles in 2015 reflects the importance of continuous improvement. Whether in sports or life, recognizing opportunities for growth, making strategic decisions, and embracing change contribute to ongoing success and excellence.

Trivia Answers

1. A) Cheryl Reeve
2. A) 2011
3. B) Maya Moore
4. B) Seimone Augustus
5. D) 2017

Unlock an even deeper appreciation for basketball with our exclusive free content: "100 Unique General Facts and Trivia Questions on Basketball." This resource is meticulously curated to enhance your understanding and enjoyment of the game. Whether you're a budding enthusiast or a seasoned fan, these facts and trivia questions will expand your knowledge, challenge your understanding, and provide hours of fun. Discover intriguing details about the sport's history, iconic players, and memorable moments that have shaped basketball as we know it today. To access this invaluable resource, simply scan the QR code provided and start your journey into the fascinating world of basketball trivia and facts.

In the world of women's basketball, no state shows more support than Connecticut. Why? Because for years, the University of Connecticut's team, the Lady Huskies, have dominated the game with graduates going on to become global stars in the WNBA. But what's the secret to their decades of success? As with most answers, this one isn't simple. It took a combination of grit, determination, discipline, consistency, and a wealth of talent among the players and coaching staff.

While programs like Duke, Notre Dame, and Tennessee have experienced their moments at the top of women's college basketball, the UConn Huskies have scripted an unparalleled narrative of victory during the past two decades.

Whether you were cheering them on early, when they were striving to carve a niche for themselves, or jumped on the bandwagon once you caught wind of their extraordinary winning streaks, the allure of donning the UConn jersey is a dream shared by hundreds of thousands of young g rls. The reasons behind this magnetic appeal are deeply embedded in the culture cultivated by Coach Geno Auriemma and his staff.

The very essence of UConn Women's Basketball can be summed up with one term: unbridled domination. The team's historic 111-game winning streak from 2014 to 2017, with 108 of those victories secured by double-digit margins, reflects the unyielding commitment to excellence.

Becoming a UConn Lady Husky entails an unwavering expectation to deliver your best performance night after night. This demand isn't just about athleticism; it extends to a holistic approach, encompassing nutrition, mental toughness, rest, and rigorous training. The athletes are sculpted not only for sporadic brilliance but for persistent excellence throughout entire seasons.

At the foundation of these remarkable winning streaks is a recruiting process that seeks players who not only can hoop, but can also possess the character and discipline required to fully immerse themselves in the UConn culture. Joining the ranks of UConn is no mere joyride; it comes with an unrelenting pressure and scrutiny, leaving no room for error.

In the recruitment process, coaches seek athletes who can withstand the constant pressures, perform under the microscope, and still deliver their best. It's about identifying individuals who thrive under the stressors of the game and emerge stronger with each challenge.

While Geno Auriemma is the face most associated with UConn Women's Basketball, his ascent to the summit is not a solo journey. A robust coaching staff, sharing the same vision of dominance, stands as a crucial pillar beside him. These key contributors play a pivotal role in nurturing players and maintaining the team's operational excellence, essential elements for a program that has claimed victory in 145 regular-season conference games from 2013 to 2022.

While the landscape of Women's College Basketball continues to evolve, witnessing an influx of competitive teams in recent years, the UConn Lady Huskies etch their legacy as an enduring force that transcends the league's temporal fluctuations. Their dominance isn't confined to a specific era; it's a testament to a culture, a relentless pursuit of excellence that withstands the test of time.

Several UConn alumni have transitioned to the professional stage, notably in the WNBA, with loyalists like Sue Bird and Diana Taurasi continuing to shine as some of the oldest and most successful names in the league. This transition emphasizes the UConn formula creating a perfect storm that has consistently propelled the team to the forefront of Women's College Basketball.

As we delve into the annals of UConn's storied history, we witness not just a team dominating a game but an institution shaping the narrative of Women's College Basketball. Whether it's the captivating tale of their early struggles or the resounding success of their recent championships, UConn's impact is indelible. The echoes of their dominance resonate not only within the confines of the basketball court but also across generations of aspiring players who dream of emulating their heroes in the storied UConn jersey.

In the grand tapestry of Women's College Basketball, UConn's narrative is not just a story of victories; it's a saga of determination, resilience, and the unwavering pursuit of greatness. From the early years when they had nothing to the present-day dominance, the UConn Lady Huskies have secured their place as in the history. Their name will forever be associated with excellence as former, current, and future players continue to thrive on and off the court.

INSPIRATIONAL QUOTES

"With the absence of pressure it's hard to do great things." - Geno Auriemma

"If I can be part of a team the rest of my life, then I'm going to be a lucky guy." - Geno Auriemma

"Bottom line, you're either a risk taker, or you're not, and if you don't take risks, you'll never win big." Geno Auriemma

"When I look back, that's probably the one thing that I'm going to remember more than anything, no so much the championships, the wins, but I think we made the Big East take women's basketball seriously. I think we made people around the country pay attention to what we were doing. Because of that, it showed a lot of people out there that there's an unbelievable game out there that people were missing." - Geno Auriemma

"They say you really don't understand what winning is. You really don't appreciate what winning is until you've had your share is losing. I think the opposite is also true. I think you can't quite fathom how much losing hurts when you have had as many chances to win." - Geno Auriemma

TRIVIA QUESTIONS

1. What is emphasized as the essence of UConn Women's Basketball culture?

A) Sporadic brilliance
B) Unbridled domination
C) Occasional victories
D) Individual achievements

2. What is a crucial factor in recruiting players to join the UConn Lady Huskies?

A) Athleticism only
B) Character and discipline
C) Joyride experience
D) Minimal pressure and scrutiny

3. Besides Geno Auriemma, what is highlighted as a crucial pillar for UConn Women's Basketball's success?

A) Alumni achievements
B) Dominant players
C) Coaching staff with the same vision
D) Ever-changing landscape

4. What is the UConn formula for success in Women's College Basketball?

A) Individual brilliance
B) A solo coaching journey
C) Culture of dominance, player buy-in, and top-tier coaching staff
D) Occasional dedication

5. How is UConn's impact described in the realm of Women's College Basketball?

A) Brief success story
B) Architects of an enduring legacy
C) A solo institution
D) A team with no impact on aspiring players

LIFE LESSONS

1. **Relentless Dedication:** The success of UConn Women's Basketball underscores the importance of relentless dedication. Athletes are expected to consistently strive to be the best, not just occasionally but every night, reflecting the value of sustained effort and commitment.

2. **Character and Discipline Matter:** The emphasis on recruiting players with not only exceptional basketball prowess but also strong character and discipline highlights the importance of qualities beyond physical abilities. This teaches the life lesson that personal character and discipline contribute significantly to long-term success.

3. **Teamwork and Shared Vision:** The success of UConn is not solely attributed to individual brilliance but also to a coaching staff with a shared vision. This emphasizes the lesson that in any pursuit, whether in sports or life, effective teamwork and alignment of goals among team members are essential for achieving greatness.

4. **Adaptability in an Ever-Changing Landscape:** The acknowledgment of the evolving landscape of Women's College Basketball teaches the importance of adaptability. Life, like sports, is dynamic, and being able to adapt to changes is a valuable skill for sustained success.

5. **Legacy Through Endurance:** UConn's enduring legacy signifies the importance of endurance and resilience. Life is filled with challenges, and the ability to persevere through struggles, setbacks, and changing circumstances is a crucial life lesson for achieving long-lasting impact and success.

Trivia Answers

1. B) Unbridled domination
2. B) Character and discipline
3. C) Coaching staff with the same vision
4. C) Culture of dominance, player buy-in, and top-tier coaching staff
5. B) Architects of an enduring legacy

LeBron Raymone James, born on December 30, 1984, in Akron, Ohio, was born into circumstances that statistically placed him behind the Eightball. Gloria James, his mother, was only 16 when she gave birth to LeBron. Unfortunately, LeBron's early years were marked by financial strife as his mother struggled to make ends meet and find a safe, secure home for her and her infant. However, amidst the hardships, a spark ignited within him—the love for basketball.

Things began looking up when, at the age of nine, LeBron's mother allowed him to move in with a prep football coach. It was here that he was first exposed to the game that would change the course of his life forever. Basketball became more than just a fun pastime; it became a refuge where he found the joy that fueled his determination to rise above the odds.

"The odds have been against me since I was five, six years old. The odds have been stacked up against me since I was an adolescent," LeBron reflected during the 2018 NBA Finals. Yet, he embraced every challenge with a smile, emphasizing, "This is not adversity. Not with the things I've been through in my life. This is fun."

LeBron's talent on the court quickly became legendary during his high school days at St. Vincent-St. Mary. It was here that the young athlete started getting noticed in a way that most high schoolers can only imagine. Several of his games were broadcast nationwide on ESPN. LeBron went on a fierce run and led the team to three state championships. He was also the first high school player to pose for the cover of Sports Illustrated, an accomplishment that garnered even more attention as LeBron prepared for the next step on his road to becoming a global superstar.

In 2003, LeBron made a mature decision, choosing to bypass college and go straight into the NBA Draft. Selected as the first overall pick by the Cleveland Cavaliers, his professional journey was underway. His stellar breakout performance won James the Rookie of the Year title, and he was only getting started.

In 2010, LeBron faced both criticism and admiration for leaving Cleveland to join the Miami Heat. Many thought the move was selfish, while others commended him for pursuing his dream to be a champion. Despite initial setbacks, he led the Heat to four consecutive NBA Finals, securing championships in 2012 and 2013. Still, he knew how much the city of Cleveland would benefit if he returned and won a championship with the team. So, he returned to Cleveland in 2014 to turn that dream into a reality.

With teammates Kyrie Irving and Kevin Love, LeBron orchestrated a historic comeback in the 2016 NBA Finals, overcoming a 3-1 deficit to secure the championship. The victory fulfilled a dream and brought joy and hope to a city longing to be recognized as a winner.

In 2018, LeBron's journey continued with a move to the Los Angeles Lakers. At an age when most players experience a decline, he defied expectations, averaging 30.0 points, 8.5 rebounds, and 7.1 assists. Even in the face of challenges and the Lakers being in 13th place, his love for the game never faltered.

"I still want to be in championship mode," LeBron declared. His dedication to continuous improvement and hunger for championships kept him on the court, still performing at an MVP-caliber level.

LeBron is also a force off the court. With over 196 million followers on social media, he uses his platform to advocate for social justice. He founded the LeBron James Family Foundation, addressing issues like police brutality and racial inequality. LeBron became the first active NBA player to achieve billionaire status.

In 2018, LeBron opened the I Promise School in Akron, a public school aimed at providing support and educational opportunities for at-risk children and their families. This commitment to education aligns with his belief in the power of knowledge to uplift communities. Additionally, LeBron founded the SpringHill Company, a production company dedicated to creating compelling content that transcends boundaries.

For many players, what LeBron is doing at this stage of his career is unimaginable. Players like Luka Dončić and Draymond Green, who have significantly fewer years in the league, express their hesitancy about playing for two decades. LeBron's dedication and longevity not only demand elite skill but also reveal a genuine love for the game.

When asked about his enduring motivation, LeBron answered, "Just my drive, my drive to be the greatest to ever play this game and inspire kids all over the world and also put myself in a position to win championships."

His journey from Akron to becoming one of the most recognizable names in professional basketball is not just a testament to his athletic prowess but also to his mental fortitude, discipline, and unyielding passion for the sport.

LeBron overcame a poverty-stricken childhood in Akron to become a global icon and NBA leading scorer. His story is as awe-inspiring as his commitment to excellence and resilience in the face of adversity. LeBron's unwavering passion for the game provides a beacon of inspiration for aspiring athletes and individuals facing challenges worldwide.

LeBron is not just rewriting the record books; he's rewriting the narrative of what an athlete can achieve on the court and beyond. The combination of elite talent, longevity, and an unyielding desire to be the best is what sets LeBron James apart as a basketball legend and prevailing symbol of motivation for all.

INSPIRATIONAL QUOTES

"Once you get on the playing field it's not about whether you're liked or not liked. All that matters is to play at a high level and do whatever it takes to help your team win. That's what it's about."

"You know, my family and friends have never been yes-men: 'Yes you're doing the right thing, you're always right.' No, they tell me when I'm wrong and that's why I've been able to stay who I am and stay humble."

"You can't be afraid to fail. It's the only way you succeed - you're not gonna succeed all the time, and I know that."

"No matter how good one individual is, it takes a whole team to win a championship."

"I always say, decision I make, I live with them. There's always ways you can correct them or ways you can do them better. At the end of the day, I live with them."

TRIVIA QUESTIONS

1. What year did LeBron James declare for the NBA Draft?

A) 2000
B) 2002
C) 2003
D) 2005

2. In which city did LeBron James win his first NBA championship?

A) Cleveland
B) Miami
C) Los Angeles
D) Golden State

3. Before joining the NBA, LeBron James played high school basketball for which team?

A) Northeast Ohio Shooting Stars
B) St. Vincent-St. Mary High School
C) Akron Wildcats
D) Cleveland Cavaliers Prep

4. How many NBA championships has LeBron James won as of 2024?

A) 2
B) 3
C) 4
D) 5

5. In addition to his basketball career, LeBron James is known for founding which school in Akron?

A) LeBron Academy
B) Akron Elite School
C) I Promise School
D) Slam Dunk High School

LIFE LESSONS

1. Resilience Overcomes Adversity: Life is full of challenges, setbacks, and unexpected obstacles. Embracing resilience allows individuals to navigate difficulties, bounce back from failures, and continue moving forward with newfound strength.

2. Continuous Learning Leads to Growth: Pursuing knowledge and personal development is a lifelong journey. Every experience, whether positive or negative, provides an opportunity to learn and grow. Embracing a mindset of continuous learning fosters personal and professional development.

3. Courage in the Face of Fear: Fear is a natural part of life, but true courage lies in facing fears and stepping out of one's comfort zone. Taking risks, confronting challenges, and embracing discomfort are essential elements in the journey toward personal and professional fulfillment.

4. Empathy Builds Meaningful Connections: Understanding and empathizing with others' experiences and perspectives fosters compassion and strengthens interpersonal relationships. Building a foundation of empathy enriches personal connections and contributes to a more compassionate and understanding society.

5. Purpose Drives Meaningful Achievements: Identifying one's purpose and aligning actions with meaningful goals provides a sense of direction and fulfillment. When individuals connect their endeavors to a deeper purpose, they are more likely to persevere through challenges and find enduring satisfaction in their accomplishments.

Trivia Answers

1. C) 2003
2. B) Miami
3. B) St. Vincent-St. Mary Fighting Irish
4. C) 4
5. C) I Promise School

The NBA has a long and storied history, but the decade that stands out is the 1980s. Often referred to as the golden era of basketball, this period saw what is debatably the league's most notable rivalry—the Boston Celtics vs. the Los Angeles Lakers. But what's even more extraordinary about the fierce competition between the two teams is the journey undertaken by the Celtics.

For a team with Lucky the Leprechaun as a mascot, they did not rely on good fortune alone to win games. Instead, the 1980s Celtics spin a tale of resilience, strategic brilliance, and unwavering commitment, a narrative that serves as a wellspring of inspiration for those hoopers seeking to carve their own path to greatness.

The saga began well before the 1980s when, in 1959, the Celtics, led by the indomitable Bill Russell, clashed with what was then the Minneapolis Lakers. The Celtics' resounding 4-0 sweep marked not only their second Finals victory but the beginning of a rivalry destined to span decades.

Over the next 12 years, Boston clinched an unparalleled 10 championship titles. This remarkable feat, orchestrated under the astute coaching of Red Auerbach, showcased the transformative power of sustained excellence and teamwork. The Celtics' eight-championship streak from 1959 to 1966 is a testament to the fact that greatness is not achieved in isolation but through collective determination and shared pursuit of a common goal.

During the Celtic's dominant winning streak, the Lakers constantly found themselves in the runner-up position. However, wavering was not a part of their strategy as their audacious and confident owner, Jack Kent Cooke, was not happy being number two to Boston.

By the time the 1980s finally rolled around, the Celtics-Lakers rivalry was on the verge of a resurgence. That's because two former college rivals were now entering the NBA, and all eyes were on them. Basketball aficionados wanted to know if Larry Bird and Earvin "Magic" Johnson would continue their adversarial relationship as professionals.

The league received an injection of new vigor as fans chose sides and rooted for their favorite to win. Some preferred Bird's low-key, laid-back but serious demeanor. In contrast, others enjoyed Johnson's flash and razzle-dazzle to the stadium. No matter which side of the ball you were on, as a basketball enthusiast, you were in for a real treat whenever these old foes met.

Johnson and Bird became the driving force that revitalized the NBA in the 1980s. Their journey unfolded on the grandest stage, with the 1984 NBA Finals serving as the first iconic showdown between the two. The grueling seven-game series showcased not only their individual brilliance but the indomitable spirit of competition that elevates not just players but the entire league.

While headlines often spotlight prolific offensive players, the 1980s Boston Celtics became one of the most feared teams due to a unique blend of defensive prowess and efficient execution of the brilliant strategies devised by the coaching staff. Head Coach KC Jones, with meticulous guidance, transformed the Celtics into a defensive juggernaut, setting the stage for their aggressive run.

The early 1980s witnessed a strategic move that set the tone for a decade of unequaled success—the trade on June 9, 1980, acquiring Robert Parish and the No. 3 pick from Golden State. This savvy maneuver secured a formidable frontcourt and laid the foundation for one of the greatest trios in the history of the NBA—Parish, Kevin McHale, and Bird.

The 1981 Eastern Conference Finals is a defining chapter in the Celtics' defensive legacy. Boston wasn't deterred by a daunting 3-1 deficit against the Philadelphia 76ers. The Celtics embarked on a remarkable comeback, winning three consecutive elimination games. The defensive tenacity displayed during this comeback epitomized the Celtics' commitment to the "we" before "me" attitude, a principle that resonates beyond the basketball court.

Their defensive efforts culminated in the 1981 NBA Finals against the Houston Rockets. The Rockets were no slouches but were also no match for the Celtics' defensive prowess. Coupled with the offensive brilliance of the Big 3, the Celtics snatched the victory from the Rockets.

The 1984 NBA Finals unfolded as an epic tale of defensive resilience, with one iconic play altering the series' trajectory. In Game 2, facing a potential 2-0 deficit against the Los Angeles

Lakers, Gerald Henderson's steal with 18 seconds remaining shifted the narrative. This defensive gem prevented a crucial loss and ignited a momentum shift that ultimately led to a Celtics' triumph in seven games.

Game-saving defensive plays like Henderson's steal symbolized the Celtics' ability to turn defensive moments into offensive triumphs, solidifying their status as a defensive juggernaut. The infamous "Heat Game" in 1984 was a testament to the Celtics' defensive resilience when faced with adverse conditions. Following a blowout loss in Game 3, Bird's call for increased physicality led to a series-altering moment in Game 4. Kevin McHale's assertive clothesline takedown of Kurt Rambis became a defining defensive play, sparking a heated encounter that ultimately tilted the series in Boston's favor.

In the present day, the Lakers and Celtics stand as the NBA franchises with the most championship wins, both boasting 17 titles. Although relatively dormant in recent years, the rivalry serves as a beacon of anticipation for fans, igniting dreams of a perfect world where Magic Johnson and Larry Bird, former rivals turned friends, sit courtside, cheering on their beloved teams.

INSPIRATIONAL QUOTES

"I don't believe in statistics. There are too many factors that can't be measured. You can't measure a ballplayer's heart." - Red Auerbach, Coach

"A team is a group of players who support one another on court and who think of the group before they think of themselves." - KC Jones, Coach

"A winner is someone who recognizes his God-given talents, works his tail to develop them into skills, and uses these skills to accomplish his goals." - Larry Bird, Small Forward/Power Forward

"Push yourself again and again. Don't give an inch until the final buzzer sounds." - Larry Bird

"I wasn't real quick, and I wasn't real strong. Some guys will just take off and it's like whoa. So I beat them with my mind and my fundamentals." - Larry Bird

TRIVIA QUESTIONS

1. Who led the Boston Celtics to their second Finals victory in 1959?

A) Larry Bird
B) Bill Russell
C) Magic Johnson
D) Kevin McHale

2. Which iconic play altered the trajectory of the 1984 NBA Finals, preventing a potential 2-0 deficit for the Boston Celtics against the Los Angeles Lakers?

A) Larry Bird's three-pointer
B) Kevin McHale's assertive clothesline takedown
C) Magic Johnson's dunk
D) Gerald Henderson's steal

3. Which coach orchestrated the Celtics' remarkable eight-championship streak from 1959 to 1966, showcasing the transformative power of sustained excellence and teamwork?

A) Red Auerbach
B) KC Jones
C) Jack Kent Cooke
D) Bill Russell

4. In the 1981 Eastern Conference Finals, the Boston Celtics faced a daunting 3-1 deficit against which team before making a remarkable comeback?

A) Houston Rockets
B) Golden State Warriors
C) Philadelphia 76ers
D) Los Angeles Lakers

5. Which trade on June 9, 1980, laid the foundation for one of the greatest trios in NBA history—Robert Parish, Kevin McHale, and Larry Bird?

A) Celtics traded with the Los Angeles Lakers
B) Celtics traded with the Golden State Warriors
C) Celtics traded with the Philadelphia 76ers
D) Celtics traded with the Houston Rockets

LIFE LESSONS

1. Resilience and Comebacks: No matter how daunting the challenges, the 1981 Eastern Conference Finals demonstrated that resilience and the ability to make comebacks are invaluable. When facing a 3-1 deficit, the Celtics didn't give up; they fought back, winning three consecutive elimination games. This teaches us the importance of perseverance and bouncing back from setbacks in our own lives.

2. Teamwork and Shared Goals: The success of the Boston Celtics, particularly during their dominant era, was built on teamwork and a shared pursuit of a common goal. The lesson here is that greatness is often achieved through collective determination and collaboration. Emphasizing the "we" before "me" attitude can lead to greater achievements in various aspects of life.

3. Strategic Decision-Making: The strategic move of acquiring Robert Parish and the No. 3 pick in 1980 showcased the importance of making informed and calculated decisions. In life, strategic thinking and well-planned decisions can lay the foundation for long-term success. Being thoughtful and strategic in our actions can lead to positive outcomes.

4. Adaptability and Turning Setbacks into Triumphs: The "Heat Game" in 1984 highlighted the Celtics' ability to turn defensive moments into offensive triumphs. Kevin McHale's assertive play, though controversial, became a defining moment that turned the series in Boston's favor. In life, being adaptable and finding opportunities within challenges can lead to unexpected triumphs.

5. Friendship and Mutual Respect: The rivalry between Larry Bird and Magic Johnson turned into a friendship off the court. This teaches us the value of mutual respect and the potential for positive relationships even in competitive environments. In life, fostering positive connections and respecting others can lead to lasting and meaningful relationships.

Trivia Answers

1. B) Bill Russell
2. D) Gerald Henderson's steal
3. A) Red Auerbach
4. C) Philadelphia 76ers
5. B) Celtics traded with the Golden State Warriors

Statistically speaking, Kareem Abdul-Jabbar is the second-highest scorer in NBA history. How did he achieve such an honor? Of course, you expect to hear the traditional answers like hard work, initiative, consistency, and a no-excuses attitude. While all of that is true, it also can be summed up in one word: Skyhook.

Now, this is not a shot you see a lot in today's NBA, and it wasn't a shot that was popular when Abdul-Jabbar used it to outscore everyone around him. But he made it his own, and it was obviously effective.

The Skyhook was a move of sheer brilliance. Abdul-Jabbar would post up against opponents, then, with the grace of a seasoned ballet dancer, deftly turn on his left shoulder and release a hook shot with his right hand. This simple move, combined with Abdul-Jabbar's extraordinarily light touch and impressive eight-foot wingspan, turned the Hall-of-Fame center into an unstoppable scoring machine.

The Skyhook was Kareem's weapon of choice and a move only a select few, like the towering Wilt Chamberlain, could hope to block. And blocking the shot was no small feat. The opponent needed a similar physical build or an extraordinary combination of willpower and athleticism to render it ineffective.

Renowned NBA figures, including Reggie Miller, have emphatically stated that the Skyhook is an irreplaceable phenomenon, a testament to Kareem's innate mastery of the shot. During a segment on NBA TV's Open Court, Miller stated, "First of all, Kareem was born with that shot. Even Magic Johnson attempted to emulate or copy it to a certain degree, but it wasn't the same Kareem Abdul-Jabbar Skyhook."

According to Miller, the Skyhook stands as a move that defies duplication. It kept defenders bewildered as they tried to find ways to keep Kareem out of the post, but it was an impossible mission.

The offensive legacy of Kareem Abdul-Jabbar extends throughout his illustrious basketball career, making him the most decorated player of his era—from his high school days to the culmination of his NBA journey. Drafted as the first overall pick in 1969, Kareem wasted no time asserting his dominance, swiftly evolving into a basketball superstar upon entering the league. Formerly known as Lew Alcindor, he showcased his scoring prowess by averaging an impressive 28.8 points in his rookie season, setting the stage for a career solidifying his status as one of the greatest scorers in basketball history. The zenith of his scoring brilliance came in his third year during the 1971-72 season, where he astoundingly averaged 34.8 points per game.

The near-unstoppable nature of the Skyhook against the centers of his era contributed to Kareem's incredible career total of 38,387 points. In the modern NBA, characterized by a relentless emphasis on speed and precision, the slow and deliberate style needed to make the Skyhook work is long gone. While contemporary big men like Nikola Jokic occasionally incorporate the hook shot into their arsenal, the Skyhook has become a relic of a bygone era.

Still, Kareem Abdul-Jabbar's Skyhook remains not only a symbol of his basketball genius but also a representation of an era when a seemingly simple yet devastatingly effective move stood as the most unstoppable force in NBA history. As the game continues to evolve, the legacy of the Skyhook endures as a testament to the enduring impact of one player's mastery of a singular, game-changing maneuver.

INSPIRATIONAL QUOTES

"Great players are willing to give up their own personal achievement for the achievement of the group. It enhances everybody."

"One man can be a crucial ingredient on a team, but one man cannot make a team."

"We can learn from the mistakes of others, whether they're kings or our parents. When we do learn those lessons, we're better equipped to make our own dreams come true."

"I think someone should explain to the child that it's OK to make mistakes. That's how we learn. When we compete, we make mistakes."

"You can't win unless you learn how to lose."

TRIVIA QUESTIONS

1. What was Kareem Abdul-Jabbar's most famous and effective offensive move?

A) Three-point shot
B) Dunk
C) Crossover dribble
D) Skyhook

2. What was required of an opponent to stop Kareem Abdul-Jabbar's Skyhook?

A) Similar physical build
B) Extraordinary willpower
C) Athleticism
D) All of the above

3. In which season did Kareem Abdul-Jabbar achieve his highest points-per-game average, showcasing his scoring brilliance?

A) 1969-70
B) 1971-72
C) 1973-74
D) 1980-81

4. What were Kareem Abdul-Jabbar's total career points in the NBA?

A) 28,596
B) 34,234
C) 38,387
D) 41,112

5. According to Reggie Miller, why is Kareem Abdul-Jabbar's Skyhook considered an irreplaceable phenomenon?

A) It requires a specific physical build.
B) It was a move only Kareem could master.
C) Magic Johnson couldn't replicate it.
D) All of the above

LIFE LESSONS

1. Innovation and Uniqueness: Just as Kareem Abdul-Jabbar's Skyhook was a unique and innovative move, embrace your individuality. Don't be afraid to develop your own path and stand out from the crowd. Your uniqueness can be your greatest strength.

2. Persistence and Mastery: Kareem's career showcases the importance of persistence and continuous improvement. Mastery of a skill, like his Skyhook, takes time and dedication. Persistently working toward your goals and mastering your craft can lead to long-term success.

3. Adaptation to Change: The disappearance of the Skyhook in modern NBA play symbolizes the game's evolution. Similarly, be open to change and adapt to new circumstances in life. The ability to evolve and embrace change is crucial for personal growth and success.

4. Legacy and Impact: Kareem Abdul-Jabbar's legacy is not just about scoring points but about the lasting impact he made on the game of basketball. Consider the impact you want to leave on the world. Strive to contribute positively to your community and leave a legacy that extends beyond personal achievements.

5. Resilience in the Face of Challenges: Kareem faced opponents who tried to block his unstoppable Skyhook. Similarly, in life, challenges and obstacles are inevitable. Cultivate resilience to bounce back from setbacks, learn from failures, and keep moving forward with determination.

Trivia Answers

1. D) Skyhook
2. D) All of the above
3. B) 1971-72
4. C) 38,387
5. D) All of the above

Unlock an even deeper appreciation for basketball with our exclusive free content: "100 Unique General Facts and Trivia Questions on Basketball." This resource is meticulously curated to enhance your understanding and enjoyment of the game. Whether you're a budding enthusiast or a seasoned fan, these facts and trivia questions will expand your knowledge, challenge your understanding, and provide hours of fun. Discover intriguing details about the sport's history, iconic players, and memorable moments that have shaped basketball as we know it today. To access this invaluable resource, simply scan the QR code provided and start your journey into the fascinating world of basketball trivia and facts.

The road to establishing a professional women's basketball league was a rocky one. While we are all now familiar with the WNBA, the Women's Professional Basketball League (WPBL) was the first to give women a shot on the national stage. Founded in 1978, the WPBL promised an exciting future for women athletes, with eight teams ready to compete in major cities across the United States.

However, despite efforts to hold the public's interest, the WPBL faced internal struggles and financial woes. During the 1980-81 season, players from the Minnesota Fillies walked off the court in protest over unpaid salaries, bringing attention to the league's internal turmoil. By the fall of 1981, the WPBL faced its inevitable demise.

So, when talks began swirling about starting another professional league for women, the skeptics came out in droves. It would take a group of dynamic players to change the minds of critics, and fortunately for the WNBA, that group of women existed.

It was 1996 and the USA Basketball Women's National Team won the Olympic gold during the summer games. These remarkable athletes were some of the first to play in the WNBA's inaugural season, which began in June of the following year.

The game that set it all off was played by the Los Angeles Sparks and New York Liberty. Played in sunny California, the nationally televised game captivated audiences across the country.

Despite a challenging starting season which ended with a 14–14 record (just missing the playoffs) the team laid the foundation for greatness. The spotlight was shining brightly on one of the brilliant athletes who helped bring home the Olympic Gold Medal, Lisa Leslie. She would prove to be a towering force and become the heart and soul of the Sparks.

The 1999 season marked a turning point as the Sparks clinched their first playoff berth with a 20–12 record. Lisa Leslie's development into a formidable player propelled the team to new heights. Although falling short in the Western Conference Finals against the Houston Comets, the Sparks ignited a passion that would soon blaze into a wildfire of success.

The year 2000 witnessed a record-breaking season for the Sparks with a remarkable 28–4 record, setting a new standard in league history. The bar of excellence was raised. Despite their outstanding regular-season performance, the Sparks would still fall to the Comets in the Western Conference Finals. The quest for greatness, however, had only just begun.

The dawn of the new millennium ushered in a golden era for Los Angeles. The 2001 season saw the arrival of Lisa Leslie's genius on the court as she walked away with the league's Most Valuable Player (MVP) award. The team soared to the top with a 28–4 regular-season record, securing their first championship by defeating the Charlotte Sting in the finals. Leslie's impressive averages of 19.5 points, 9.6 rebounds, and 2.3 blocks per game epitomized the Sparks' commitment to excellence.

Building on their triumph, the Sparks achieved a historic back-to-back championship in 2002. But that wasn't the only record that would be shattered when Leslie became the first woman in the league to dunk the ball during a game. The team's dominance continued with a 25–7 regular-season record, sweeping through the playoffs and clinching the title against the New York Liberty. The Sparks had solidified their place as frontrunners in women's basketball.

These were exciting times for women's basketball. Young girls everywhere now had a group of ladies they could model themselves after, leading the charge in professional sports.

Leslie's retirement in 2009 marked the end of an era, but the Sparks, true to their legacy, embraced new talent. In 2012, the team secured the top pick in the draft, selecting Nneka Ogwumike. Paired with Candace Parker, the dynamic duo propelled the Sparks back into the limelight, ultimately winning the franchise's third championship in 2016.

The Sparks' impact extended beyond the court, transcending wins and losses. In 2017, Spark into S.T.E.M. launched to provide girls living in at-risk neighborhoods with science, technology, engineering, and math. The team also regularly partners with nonprofits and other community organizations throughout Southern California to give back.

As we stand on the shoulders of giants like Lisa Leslie, the Los Angeles Sparks' journey becomes a source of inspiration. Their legacy reminds us that success is not measured solely by victories but by the resilience to rise after each defeat. The Sparks continue to illuminate the path for future generations, embodying the spirit of triumph against all odds in the evolving landscape of women's basketball.

INSPIRATIONAL QUOTES

"Well, the first quality of being a good leader is you have to be able to follow. See, a good leader can't just be the leader all the time, I have to be able to follow." - t"The one thing I learned about myself going back and watching tapes of all the losses that we've had is that I'm physically capable of doing this and dominating the game, but the mental part was not there. I don't know if it comes with age, but I had to learn to be mentally tough." - Lisa Leslie

"Everyone talks about age, but it's not about age, it's about work ethic. Winning never gets old." - Lisa Leslie

"Believe in yourself, even when other's doubt you." - Candace Parker, Forward

"Success is not determined by your circumstances but by your determination." - Candace Parker

TRIVIA QUESTIONS

1. In which year did the Women's Professional Basketball League (WPBL) face its demise?

A) 1985
B) 1981
C) 1990
D) 1975

2. Who was the MVP (Most Valuable Player) in the WNBA's inaugural season in 1997?

A) Lisa Leslie
B) Candace Parker
C) Nneka Ogwumike
D) Diana Taurasi

3. Which team did the Los Angeles Sparks defeat to secure their first WNBA championship in 2001?

A) New York Liberty
B) Houston Comets
C) Charlotte Sting
D) Minnesota Fillies

4. Who became the first woman in the WNBA to dunk the ball during a game?

A) Candace Parker
B) Nneka Ogwumike
C) Lisa Leslie
D) Diana Taurasi

5. In what year did the Los Angeles Sparks win their franchise's third championship with the dynamic duo of Nneka Ogwumike and Candace Parker?

A) 2010
B) 2016
C) 2005
D) 2018

LIFE LESSONS

1. Resilience in the Face of Setbacks: The story of the Women's Professional Basketball League (WPBL) and its eventual demise teaches us the importance of resilience. Despite facing internal struggles and financial troubles, the failure of the WPBL did not deter the subsequent efforts to establish a women's professional basketball league. The eventual success of the WNBA highlights the resilience required to overcome setbacks and pursue a vision despite initial failures.

2. Courage to Challenge Skepticism: The skeptics who doubted the feasibility of another women's professional basketball league could have hindered progress. However, the success of the WNBA shows that a determined group of individuals, in this case, dynamic players from the USA Basketball Women's National Team, had the courage to challenge skepticism. The lesson here is to pursue one's goals despite doubters and naysayers.

3. Teamwork and Leadership: The journey of the Los Angeles Sparks emphasizes the significance of teamwork and leadership. While individual brilliance, such as Lisa Leslie's contributions, played a crucial role, it was the collective effort of the team that laid the foundation for success. The arrival of players like Nneka Ogwumike and Candace Parker later on showcases how successful teams evolve by embracing new talent and fostering a strong sense of teamwork.

4. Commitment to Excellence: The Sparks' commitment to excellence, as seen in their pursuit of championships and record-breaking performances, serves as a life lesson. Regardless of initial challenges or setbacks, consistent dedication to high standards and continuous improvement can lead to long-term success. The Sparks' journey encourages individuals to set a high bar for themselves and persevere in the pursuit of excellence.

5. Community Engagement and Social Responsibility: Beyond the victories on the court, the Los Angeles Sparks' commitment to community engagement and social responsibility through initiatives like Spark into S.T.E.M. underscores the broader impact of sports organizations. The lesson here is that success is not only measured by wins and losses but also by the positive influence a team can have on the community. The Sparks' legacy teaches the importance of giving back and using success as a platform to contribute to the well-being of society.

Trivia Answers

1. B) 1981
2. A) Lisa Leslie
3. C) Charlotte Sting
4. C) Lisa Leslie
5. B) 2016

This story begins in the faraway bustling neighborhood of Sepolia located in Athens, Greece. It was here that a young boy named Giannis Antetokounmpo embarked on a journey that would defy the odds and rewrite the narrative of his humble beginnings. Parents Charles and Veronica were migrants from Lagos, Nigeria. The Antetokounmpo family faced the challenges of undocumented status in a land that didn't offer birthright citizenship, making life in Sepolia difficult.

Charles and Veronica struggled to secure steady employment, but remained undeterred by their circumstances. Taking matters into their own hands, they hit the streets, often with their sons in tow. Giannis and his brothers, Thanasis, Kostas, and Alex, sold items to put food on the table. Some days, Giannis's wouldn't eat his first meal until 11pm, highlighting the harsh reality of their daily struggles.

It was a chance encounter with Spiros Velliniatis, a Greek man with no prior connection to the Antetokounmpos, that would change the course of Giannis's and his family's life forever. Spiros, captivated by the athleticism he saw in the young boys, steered them toward Filathlitikos, a modest basketball club in Zografou.

Transitioning from the streets of Sepolia to the basketball court was not without its challenges. Without proper citizenship documents, Giannis and his family faced obstacles in moving to the top-tier league. However, against all odds, a video of Giannis caught the attention of Greek agents, who, in turn, introduced him to the international NBA scouting community.

At first, the NBA scouts were skeptical because of the video's poor quality and the unimpressive league Giannis played in. But what they weren't skeptical about was Giannis's raw athleticism, speed, and court vision. These elements set him apart from the rest, and the Milwaukee Bucks took a chance on Giannis in the 2013 NBA Draft, selecting him at #15 despite the uncertainties surrounding his citizenship and ability to travel.

Giannis made it to Milwaukee, where expectations were low for the struggling franchise. No one knew anything about him yet, and this anonymity allowed him to grow and develop without the pressures and expectations many big names face upon entering the league. It was here he would learn how to weightlift and adapt his game to meet NBA standards.

His journey was also full of emotional challenges. Guilt-ridden over his newfound wealth, Giannis often turned into a strict money saver as he envisioned a better life for his family. While he traveled and was able to sleep in luxury hotels with a plethora of accommodations, his family's circumstances weighed heavy on his mind. He would choose to sleep on the floor instead of on the plush mattress covered in the finest bed linens, a testament to the discomfort he felt with his changed circumstances.

His deep connection with family remained at the core of his identity. The Antetokounmpo brothers, bonded by their challenging upbringing, became inseparable. Giannis, now a leader and provider for his family, faced the tragic loss of his father, Charles, mid-career, reinforcing the importance of family in his life.

Giannis's success transformed Milwaukee into a city that embraced him genuinely and wholeheartedly. The Fiserv Forum became synonymous with the "House That Giannis Built," and the city found in him a new representative. Milwaukee fans, accustomed to being overlooked, reveled in having a global superstar who not only loved their city but affirmed its goodness and work ethic.

Giannis's journey from an undocumented migrant in Sepolia to an NBA champion is a testament to resilience, hard work, and the power of dreams. His story, often doubted and underestimated, challenges preconceptions about who can be the face of the league. Despite facing criticism about his accent and background, Giannis remains unapologetically true to himself and his roots.

His voice, shaped by experiences of poverty, migration, and success, is poised to impact broader issues, from racial identity to social justice. The "Greek Freak" has evolved from a shy rookie to a global basketball icon, and his journey is far from over. As he navigates the complexities of fame, family, and legacy, Giannis Antetokounmpo continues to inspire not just aspiring basketball players but anyone who dares to dream against the odds.

INSPIRATIONAL QUOTES

"Whatever I try to do, I always try to give it my best and try to be a killer because, at the end of the day, if you don't work hard, you are not going to get food on your table."

"I see myself as a student. Trying to learn everything."

"If you are going to do something, you have to do it for yourself, and that's what I try to do. I try to be authentic and try to be original..."

"It's such a long season, and there's so many games, so many trips, you've got to build habits and be consistent with what you do."

"You can just never forget where you came from."

TRIVIA QUESTIONS

1. What was the name of the basketball club in Zografou that Spiros Velliniatis steered Giannis and his brothers toward?

A) Zephyr Basketball Club
B) Filathlitikos
C) Olympus Hoops
D) Sepolia Slam Dunkers

2. In the 2013 NBA Draft, which pick did the Milwaukee Bucks use to select Giannis Antetokounmpo?

A) #1
B) #5
C) #10
D) #15

3. Despite initial skepticism from NBA scouts, what qualities in Giannis caught their attention?

A) Exceptional three-point shooting
B) Raw athleticism, speed, and court vision
C) Exceptional dunking ability
D) Superior defensive skills

4. What did Giannis prioritize over sleeping in luxury hotels during his early NBA career?

A) Fine dining
B) Expensive clothing
C) Money saving for his family
D) Exotic vacations

5. What tragic event reinforced the importance of family in Giannis's life?

A) Giannis's career-ending injury
B) Loss of his father, Charles
C) Struggle to adapt to NBA standards
D) Criticism about his accent and background

LIFE LESSONS

1. Resilience Triumphs Over Circumstances: Giannis's journey from an undocumented migrant facing daily struggles to an NBA champion highlights the power of resilience. Despite the odds stacked against him, he overcame challenges, showcasing that a determined spirit can triumph over difficult circumstances.

2. Embrace Opportunities, Regardless of Origin: Giannis's chance encounter with Spiros Velliniatis led him to Filathlitikos, setting the stage for his basketball career. This underscores the importance of seizing unexpected opportunities, even if they come from unfamiliar or unlikely sources.

3. Believe in Your Unique Abilities: NBA scouts initially doubted Giannis due to the quality of the video and the league he played in. However, his raw athleticism, speed, and court vision set him apart. The lesson here is to believe in and leverage one's unique strengths, even when others may be skeptical or critical.

4. Family Remains the Core of Identity: Despite achieving global fame and success, Giannis remained deeply connected to his family. The tragic loss of his father reinforced the importance of family bonds. This teaches us that, amid life's challenges and achievements, maintaining strong connections with loved ones is a grounding and essential aspect of personal identity.

5. Stay True to Yourself and Your Roots: Giannis faced criticism about his accent and background, but he remained unapologetically true to himself and his roots. His authenticity and pride in his identity challenge preconceptions, teaching us the importance of staying true to our core values and embracing our unique backgrounds despite external pressures.

Trivia Answers

1. B) Filathlitikos
2. D) #15
3. B) Raw athleticism, speed, and court vision
4. C) Money saving for his family
5. B) Loss of his father, Charles

In July 2016, one of the most iconic figures, Tim Duncan, also known as "The Big Fundamental," retired from basketball. In this chapter, we embark on a journey through the life and career of this extraordinary athlete, exploring the indomitable leadership, unwavering humility, and unparalleled success that defined Tim Duncan's impact on the game and beyond.

Tim Duncan's story begins on April 25th, 1976, in Christiansted, St. Croix, where, from an early age, it was obvious to the adults around him that Tim possessed innate basketball talent. As a high school player, he won the US Virgin Islands Player of the Year three times and led his team through two undefeated seasons. That is when college scouts began paying attention to the young phenom. Duncan ended up at Wake Forest University, where he clinched the ACC Player of the Year title twice and snagged the Naismith College Basketball Player of the Year as a senior.

Pulling back the lens to gain a wide view of Tim Duncan's illustrious career, you'll find a narrative of consistency and excellence. Averaging 19 points, 10 rebounds, and three assists per game, Duncan boasted a staggering 50% shooting accuracy, securing his place among the elite basketball players. With 13 NBA All-Star appearances, five NBA Championships, and two NBA MVP awards, his accolades mirror the unparalleled legacy he crafted over his 19 seasons with the San Antonio Spurs.

Duncan's basketball acumen went beyond mere statistics. His on-court presence was a harmonious blend of offensive prowess and defensive mastery. A walking triple-double threat, his basketball IQ and court vision were unparalleled. Whether threading the needle with a precise pass or grabbing a crucial rebound, Duncan's decision-making was consistently impeccable.

Defensively, Tim Duncan's impact was nothing short of legendary. His long arms and quick footwork allowed him to guard players across multiple positions, forcing opponents to recalibrate their offensive strategies. His ability to anticipate moves and stay one step ahead solidified his status as one of the greatest big-man defenders in the annals of NBA history.

Duncan's leadership was the bedrock of the San Antonio Spurs' success. Nicknamed "The Stone Buddha" for his stoic demeanor, he eschewed the flamboyance often associated with star athletes. Instead, he led by example, inspiring teammates with his unparalleled work ethic and unwavering commitment to teamwork. His non-vocal and non-emotional approach earned him the respect of peers, creating an environment where opponents hesitated to engage in trash talk, knowing Duncan's quiet resolve spoke volumes.

Many who played in the league against Duncan recall trying to trash-talk him and not receiving the intended response from the gentle giant. Instead, he would laugh at his opponents, which annoyed them more. Rather than taking Duncan out of his game, the big man pulled a reverse move and left the other side scratching their head.

Kevin Garnett, a notorious trash talker, says Duncan would not talk trash in full sentences. Instead, he would congratulate his opponent on a rebound and say things like, "Good job" or "Nice rebound," which was more infuriating.

DeMarcus Cousins recalls one game night when he was doing well against Duncan. In fact, so well, he decided it was the perfect time to start talking junk and call Duncan vile names. Duncan simply smiled at Cousins and then proceeded to drop 16 points straight without saying one word.

Duncan set the tone for the team and exemplified what it means to keep your emotions under control. So many players can be taken out of their element by a few mean, hurtful words. Duncan was well aware that the other team would employ such tactics and undoubtedly used the knowledge he gained while studying psychology in college to combat the strategy.

Off the court, Tim Duncan's leadership extended beyond the locker room. A mentor to younger players, he emphasized the importance of teamwork and cohesion. His impact wasn't confined to the hardwood; it resonated within the community. Duncan's philanthropy extended to local charities, and his initiative, the Tim Duncan Foundation, helps fund nonprofits poised to assist with health awareness, research, education, and youth sports.

The Spurs recognized Duncan as a leader and a player who deftly avoided the pitfalls of arrogance and toxicity. As an employee, recognition within the team became a crucial element for long-term success, echoing Duncan's own journey.

While Tim Duncan's retirement marked the end of an era on the court, his influence continues to reverberate throughout the NBA. Duncan's commitment to fundamentals and team culture stood as a guiding light in an era of high-flying athleticism and flashy showmanship. Teams across the league sought to emulate the success of the San Antonio Spurs. Still, they invariably acknowledged a crucial missing piece—they didn't have Tim Duncan.

INSPIRATIONAL QUOTES

"The time when there is no one there to feel sorry for you or to cheer for you is when a player is made."

"I believed in what I was. I didn't believe that would translate into any of the five championships. But I knew that I could affect the game."

"When you have to stop and think about things is when they go wrong."

"I've been competitive from day one. It's in my nature. Whether people recognize that or not, I don't know how they can't. I'm not gonna go out there and try to hurt somebody or win by all means. But if it's up in the air, I'm gonna try harder than you to get it done."

"Good, better, best. Never let it rest until your good is better and your better is best."

TRIVIA QUESTIONS

1. Where and when was Tim Duncan born?

A) Kingston, Jamaica, 1974
B) Christiansted, St. Croix, 1976
C) Miami, Florida, 1980
D) San Antonio, Texas, 1982

2. How many times did Tim Duncan win the US Virgin Islands Player of the Year award in high school?

A) Once
B) Twice
C) Three times
D) Four times

3. Which university did Tim Duncan attend, and how many times did he win the ACC Player of the Year title while playing college basketball?

A) University of North Carolina–Chapel Hill, once
B) Duke University, twice
C) Wake Forest University, twice
D) Kentucky University, three times

4. How many NBA All-Star appearances did Tim Duncan make during his career?

A) 10
B) 13
C) 15
D) 18

5. What nickname did Tim Duncan earn for his stoic demeanor, and how did he handle trash talk on the basketball court?

A) The Big Fundamental; he responded with aggressive comebacks.
B) The Stone Buddha; he would laugh at opponents' trash talk.
C) The Silent Assassin; he would ignore trash talk completely.
D) The Gentle Giant; he would engage in verbal sparring with opponents.

LIFE LESSONS

1. Consistency and Excellence Yield Success: Tim Duncan's career is a testament to the power of consistency and excellence. By maintaining high standards in his performance on and off the court, Duncan achieved unparalleled success over his 19 seasons in the NBA.

2. Leadership by Example: Duncan's leadership style was characterized by leading through example rather than vocal dominance. His stoic demeanor and unwavering work ethic inspired teammates and earned him respect. The lesson here is that actions often speak louder than words in leadership.

3. Maintain Humility Despite Achievements: Despite numerous accolades and championships, Tim Duncan remained humble throughout his career. This humility, coupled with his quiet resolve, allowed him to avoid the pitfalls of arrogance and toxicity. The lesson is to stay grounded and humble, regardless of personal achievements.

4. Embrace Challenges and Stay Calm Under Pressure: Duncan's ability to stay calm under pressure, whether facing opponents on the court or dealing with trash talk, showcases the importance of maintaining composure in challenging situations. Learning to control one's emotions and make sound decisions in the face of adversity is a valuable life lesson.

5. Contribute Beyond Yourself: Tim Duncan's impact extended beyond the basketball court. His commitment to teamwork and community involvement, as seen through his mentorship of younger players and philanthropic efforts, emphasizes the importance of contributing positively to the broader community. The lesson here is to consider the impact one can have beyond personal success.

Trivia Answers

1. B) Christiansted, St. Croix, 1976
2. C) Three times
3. C) Wake Forest University, twice
4. B) 13
5. B) The Stone Buddha; he would laugh at opponents' trash talk.

Elephants are large, majestic creatures that don't have many enemies in the wild due to their size. That makes them one of the most unbothered mammals on Earth. But just imagine a mouse darting around, nibbling at the elephant's ankles. The poor elephant doesn't stand a chance against the smaller, quicker, nimbler opponent. There are times when being physically bigger is a disadvantage.

Now, that may sound wrong, especially when it comes to basketball. It's always seen as a big man's game as teams seek to gain tall, strong players. But every once in a while, a small man comes in and shakes things up. Muggsy Bogues was one of those men.

Standing at just 5'3", Tyrone Curtis "Muggsy" Bogues emerged as the shortest player ever to be drafted into the NBA, leaving a permanent mark on the game of basketball.

Growing up in the projects on the rough and tumble streets of Baltimore, Maryland, he would have to overcome several adversities to make it out. The playgrounds, where children escape reality and have fun for a few hours, were full of children who poked fun at Muggsy's size.

"The kids were cruel, and it was hurtful. I got picked on a lot," recalls Muggsy. Battling through the cruelty of his peers, he found solace and support in his mother, a beacon of unwavering love amid the chaos. He would go home and tell his mother what the other kids were saying, and being 4'11" herself, she knew just what to say to keep her son's spirits up.

When Muggsy was just 5 years old, he quickly found out what it meant to be in the wrong place at the wrong time when hit by a stray buckshot. As if that wasn't horrible enough, he also witnessed a man be beaten to death. But, at 7 years old, fate intervened in the form of Leon Howard, the Director of the recreation center in Muggsy's projects.

Howard became Muggsy's guiding light, teaching him the fundamentals of basketball and instilling a tenacious defensive style that would later become his trademark. Muggsy's quick darts and steals earned him the nickname "Muggsy"—a testament to his ability to mug opponents of possession.

He took his talents to Dunbar High School, where he played under the mentorship of Coach Bob Wade. Muggsy found his footing in a highly talented unit, including future NBA stars David Wingate, Reggie Williams, and Reggie Lewis. The team's stellar chemistry, coupled with Wade's emphasis on humility, propelled them to perfection. The team's record was 29-0 in Muggsy's junior year and a flawless 31-0 in his senior year, securing the top rank in the nation.

Muggsy's journey continued at Wake Forest University, where he honed his skills, graduating as the Atlantic Coast Conference leader in steals and assists. His standout performance against 5'7" Spud Webb in a nationally televised game showcased his prowess.

uggsy's college years not only solidified his basketball prowess but also garnered international recognition. Playing for the USA national team in the 1986 FIBA World Championship, he clinched the gold medal under the guidance of Coach Lute Olson.

The pivotal moment came in 1987 when Muggsy Bogues, standing 16½ inches shorter than the average NBA player, heard his name called at the NBA draft. Joining the Washington Bullets as the 12th overall pick, he defied expectations, leading the team in both assists and steals in his rookie year.

Muggsy's impact reached new heights with the Charlotte Hornets, an expansion team he led to the playoffs three times. His tenacity on both ends of the court made him a fan favorite, challenging giants like Michael Jordan and Patrick Ewing. Despite a height difference of 16.5 inches with his teammate Manute Bol, Muggsy's chemistry and fearless play were evident.

In the 1993 playoffs against the New York Knicks and a face-off with Patrick Ewing, Muggsy showcased his defensive prowess, stealing a shot and driving the ball down the court. Even Michael Jordan found himself frustrated by the vexing Hornets guard in the 1995 playoffs, cementing Muggsy's fearless and pesky presence on the court.

Muggsy also had fun off the court, making cameo appearances in movies and TV series, including Space Jam and Saturday Night Live. His versatility showcased his multidimensional personality, making him more than an iconic basketball figure.

A brief stint with the Golden State Warriors and the Toronto Raptors marked the latter part of Muggsy's playing career. Chronic knee injuries presented challenges, but his spirit prevailed. Ultimately, he retired in 2001, leaving an enduring legacy as the all-time leader in assists and steals for the Charlotte Hornets.

Postretirement, Muggsy's commitment to the game endured. Coaching the Charlotte Sting in the WNBA and mentoring at the United Faith Christian Academy, he shared his wealth of knowledge. His insights into the different playing styles of men and women shed light on the game's nuances.

Muggsy Bogues now resides in Charlotte, serving as a brand ambassador for the Hornets and the NBA. Through the Muggsy Bogues Family Foundation, he extends a helping hand to underserved communities, providing access to education and job training.

Muggsy Bogues' journey from the tough streets of Baltimore to the pinnacle of professional basketball exemplifies his will to succeed and unwavering spirit. His story transcends the court, inspiring countless individuals to overcome obstacles and pursue their dreams despite the odds stacked against them. Muggsy's legacy lives on, a testament to the transformative power of passion, perseverance, and the relentless pursuit of excellence.

INSPIRATIONAL QUOTES

"As a small guard, you need to understand how you impact the game and make sure you impact it in the way that you can showcase your talent on the floor and having that understanding of the game."

"You've got to have the skills. You've got to have a great attitude because, if you don't, nobody will want to deal with you."

"I understood my path and what I meant to the game and what I mean to kids. Not only kids, but individuals around the world. Folks that didn't think that the game was meant for smaller people. For me, I always felt that, tall or small, the game was for all."

"That's what you want to keep sharing with the players in today's world: knowing that you represent yourself and your family each time you step on the court and to be the best at it because you never know where it leads to after it's all said and done."

"Being able to compete against the best, having success against the best, and to be included with the best - that's something I really relished whenever I got on the court."

TRIVIA QUESTIONS

1. What is Muggsy Bogues' height?

A) 6'1"
B) 5'7"
C) 5'3"
D) 6'5"

2. In which NBA team was Muggsy Bogues selected as the 12th overall pick in the draft?

A) Charlotte Hornets
B) Washington Bullets
C) Golden State Warriors
D) Toronto Raptors

3. Muggsy Bogues played a pivotal defensive role in the 1993 playoffs against which team?

A) Los Angeles Lakers
B) Boston Celtics
C) New York Knicks
D) Chicago Bulls

4. During his college years, Muggsy Bogues graduated as the leader in steals and assists in which basketball conference?

A) Big East Conference
B) Atlantic Coast Conference
C) Southeastern Conference
D) Pac-12 Conference

5. What role did Leon Howard play in Muggsy Bogues' life?

A) College Coach
B) NBA Teammate
C) Director of the recreation center
D) Childhood friend and mentor

LIFE LESSONS

1. Resilience in the Face of Adversity: Muggsy faced numerous challenges, from being taunted for his size to surviving a stray buckshot incident as a child. His ability to overcome adversity showcases the importance of resilience and perseverance in the face of difficulties.

2. The Power of Mentorship: Leon Howard, the Director of the recreation center, played a pivotal role in Muggsy's life by becoming his mentor. This highlights the significance of positive role models and mentors in shaping one's character, providing guidance, and helping navigate life's challenges.

3. Humility and Teamwork: Muggsy's high school team achieved perfection with a 31-0 record, emphasizing the importance of humility and teamwork. Coach Bob Wade's emphasis on humility contributed to the team's success, showcasing how working collaboratively and staying humble can lead to achievements.

4. Defying Expectations: Muggsy's success in the NBA, despite being significantly shorter than his peers, teaches the valuable lesson of defying societal expectations. His story encourages individuals to embrace their unique qualities and overcome preconceived limitations.

5. Community Engagement and Giving Back: Muggsy's commitment to the community, both during and after his playing career, exemplifies the importance of giving back. Through the Muggsy Bogues Family Foundation, he contributes to underserved communities, emphasizing the transformative power of education and job training.

Trivia Answers

1. C) 5'3"
2. B) Washington Bullets
3. C) New York Knicks
4. B) Atlantic Coast Conference
5. C) Director of the recreation center

Unlock an even deeper appreciation for basketball with our exclusive free content: "100 Unique General Facts and Trivia Questions on Basketball." This resource is meticulously curated to enhance your understanding and enjoyment of the game. Whether you're a budding enthusiast or a seasoned fan, these facts and trivia questions will expand your knowledge, challenge your understanding, and provide hours of fun. Discover intriguing details about the sport's history, iconic players, and memorable moments that have shaped basketball as we know it today. To access this invaluable resource, simply scan the QR code provided and start your journey into the fascinating world of basketball trivia and facts.

The NBA witnessed an unexpected surge in popularity in China. That rise can be directly attributed to Yao Ming, a towering figure who made an instant impact. Author Brook Larmer aptly captures the essence of Yao's duality, stating, "Yao, on the one hand, is this great symbol of China's modern advancement, a commercial icon that can stride across the Pacific and play the role of a bridge between East and West."

Yao's journey from being a standout player in China to an eight-season NBA All-Star and the runner-up in the 2002-03 Rookie of the Year reflects meticulous planning by the Chinese government. Standing at an imposing height of 7'6", Yao became a strategic asset, carefully nurtured within a system that combines sports and discipline.

Yao's athletic prowess can be traced back to China's Sports Commission, established in 1952, which meticulously selected and trained potential athletes. This government-led initiative provided training and also covered living expenses, education, and post-sports career support.

Born in 1980, Yao Ming's exceptional height set him apart from an early age. But his growth spurt was expected, seeing as his paternal grandfather was the tallest man in Shanghai, and both Yao's parents were over 6 feet tall. Despite his initial lack of interest, his destiny was already predetermined.

Yao's upbringing involved rigorous training, strict rules, and a singular focus on basketball. The system even included mysterious concoctions aimed at boosting height, which resulted in 6'1" Yao at age 12.

Yao's professionalism and dedication eventually led him to excel in the Chinese Basketball Association (CBA), notably with the Shanghai Sharks. His achievements, including a historic victory in 1997-98, marked a turning point as dreams of making it in the NBA began to take root in Yao's mind.

After intense negotiations, Yao Ming was finally drafted by the Houston Rockets in 2002. Yao's impact on the league was immense, and he soon became an eight-time NBA All-Star. Yao was also inducted into the Naismith Memorial Basketball Hall of Fame in 2016.

The tales of Yao Ming's basketball prowess are as numerous as they are heartwarming, all echoing a common them—a giant of a man with an even larger heart, infectious generosity, and a sense of humor that overshadowed his towering stature.

The origin story of Yao's NBA journey takes us back to the astute coaching of Rudy Tomjanovich, affectionately known as Coach T. In the pre-Yao era, the Rockets struggled, winning a mere 28 games and missing the playoffs. The team's fortunes changed dramatically with Yao's arrival, a transformation witnessed by fans who vividly recall billboards adorned with the word "FRANCHISE." The path to greatness, however, started with Coach T's stern advice to work on their game during the off-season.

The pivotal moment came when Steve Francis, a key player for the Rockets, first laid eyes on Yao's game tape. The awe-inspiring footage revealed a player of unprecedented size and skill, effortlessly shooting three-pointers and showcasing remarkable athleticism. Francis found himself representing the Rockets at the draft lottery, securing the chance to draft Yao with the top pick.

As Yao entered the NBA fishbowl, becoming a global sensation, his impact on and off the court became evident. Tracy McGrady, who joined the Rockets in 2004, initially worried about communication barriers with the towering center. To his surprise, Yao spoke English and had a remarkable sense of humor. McGrady recalls the uniqueness of Yao's size and skills, emphasizing his incredible insight into the game and his impact on the sport's global popularity.

One cherished memory of Yao, etched in the mind of a Rockets fan, stands out amidst the victories and defeats. It wasn't a triumphant moment in the win column but rather a testament to Yao's incredible skills and resilience. In a game against the Blazers, Yao faced double coverage, with both defenders guarding him tightly. Undeterred, he executed a turnaround jumper with sublime precision, even drawing a foul. The ensuing swish from the free-throw line gave the Rockets the lead, showcasing his basketball prowess and unyielding spirit.

A singular talent, he propelled the Rockets to a 22-game winning streak, making them one of the league's most relevant teams during his peak. Yet, despite Herculean efforts, the team never reached the Conference Finals.

Beyond the wins and losses, Yao's focus remained on making the world a better place. From combating the illegal Chinese ivory market to spreading basketball to remote corners of the globe, Yao's endeavors extended far beyond the basketball court. His internal light and peace touched everyone he encountered, leaving an enduring mark.

Postretirement, Yao continues to be a significant figure in Chinese society, earning a bachelor's degree, owning the Shanghai Sharks, and participating in political activities. His role as the president of the Chinese Basketball Association is perfect as he not only knows the sport inside and out, but he has become a respected global figure.

In essence, Yao Ming's remarkable journey symbolizes more than just his individual success; it represents the intricate interplay between sports and the modernization of China. As a bridge between East and West, Yao's legacy extends beyond the basketball court, embodying the complexities of a nation at the crossroads of tradition and progress.

INSPIRATIONAL QUOTES

"A good leader must be fair."

"Basketball, in America, is like a culture. It is like a foreigner learning a new language... If you're going to learn a new language, you can't try to be perfect. You'll stop yourself from talking. You just have to let go."

"Sport is the best means of communication between people from different religions and countries."

"Sports teach you how to be quick. Injuries teach you how to slow down."

"I think I'll stick to what I'm used to, my principles, and that is team Number 1 and individual Number 2."

TRIVIA QUESTIONS

1. What was Yao Ming's height?

A) 6'5"
B) 7'2"
C) 7'6"
D) 8'0"

2. Which NBA team drafted Yao Ming in 2002?

A) Los Angeles Lakers
B) Chicago Bulls
C) Houston Rockets
D) Golden State Warriors

3. What key advice did Coach Rudy Tomjanovich give the Rockets players before Yao Ming's arrival?

A) Focus on marketing
B) Work on their game during the off-season
C) Ignore the critics
D) Concentrate on defense

4. Who represented the Houston Rockets at the draft lottery when they secured the chance to draft Yao Ming with the top pick?

A) Tracy McGrady
B) Steve Francis
C) Rudy Tomjanovich
D) Yao Ming himself

5. In a memorable game against the Blazers, what move did Yao Ming execute to showcase his basketball prowess?

A) Slam dunk
B) Three-pointer
C) Turnaround jumper
D) No-look pass

LIFE LESSONS

1. Dedication and Professionalism Lead to Success: Yao Ming's success in basketball and beyond is attributed to his unwavering dedication and professionalism. Regardless of challenges, maintaining a strong work ethic and staying committed to one's goals can pave the way to success.

2. Embrace Diversity and Overcome Communication Barriers: Yao Ming's ability to bridge cultural gaps and communicate effectively in English despite his towering stature highlights the importance of embracing diversity. Overcoming communication barriers fosters understanding and collaboration, contributing to personal and professional growth.

3. Resilience in the Face of Adversity: Yao Ming's resilience, as demonstrated in the game against the Blazers, teaches us to face adversity with strength and determination. Life is filled with challenges, but overcoming them with resilience can lead to triumphs and personal growth.

4. Use Success as a Platform for Positive Change: Beyond his basketball career, Yao Ming used his success as a platform to make a positive impact on the world. Engaging in philanthropy, addressing social issues, and contributing to positive change exemplify how success can be a catalyst for making a meaningful difference in society.

5. Balancing Tradition and Progress: Yao Ming's journey embodies the delicate balance between tradition and progress. Understanding and respecting one's roots while embracing modern opportunities is crucial for personal and societal growth. Striking this balance can lead to a fulfilling and harmonious life journey.

Trivia Answers

1. C) 7'6"
2. C) Houston Rockets
3. B) Work on their game during the off-season
4. B) Steve Francis
5. C) Turnaround jumper

When you hear the name Shaquille O'Neal, what immediately comes to mind? Is it the jaw-dropping dunks that shattered backboards across the USA? Or is it the vibrant, warm, and sometimes mischievous smile that flashes across his easily recognizable face?

Shaquille O'Neal, a name that resonates far beyond the basketball court, embarked on a journey that not only defined an era of dominance but showcased a versatility that transcended the confines of sports. This is the epic tale of a man who evolved from a playful giant into an icon of unparalleled influence, creating a legacy that will last long after he is gone.

From the animated charm of auto insurance commercials to gracing the cover of Frosted Flakes boxes, Shaq's larger-than-life persona reached those who had never watched a basketball game. The executive roles at Papa John's the Icy Hot commercials, and let's not forget the spirited, light-hearted banter with Charles Barkley on TNT's "Inside the NBA" presented a multifaceted individual. Shaq isn't just a basketball player—he's a charismatic entertainer who brings joy to audiences worldwide.

If you want to truly comprehend the greatness of Shaq, you must start with his exploits on the court. Beyond the playful demeanor, Shaq was a punishing athlete known as "The Diesel" who not only dunked but redefined dunking itself. The iconic play against the New York Knicks on March 25, 1999, is a testament to his power and skill, a combination of ruthless efficiency and a dash of theatricality. Shaq wasn't merely playing basketball; he was orchestrating a symphony of dominance and entertainment that resonated with fans worldwide.

This is how it went: O'Neal catches a pass in the post from Kobe Bryant and begins to overpower Knicks center Chris Dudley. With lightning speed, before Dudley can react, he finds himself beneath the rim as O'Neal elegantly spins to face the basket, setting the stage for a thunderous dunk. In an almost cinematic sequence, Dudley's face inadvertently collides with Shaq's imposing torso.

O'Neal, maintaining the signature style of his Dunkman logo, extends his legs outward, reminiscent of his iconic brand image. At the same time, Dudley clings desperately to O'Neal's legs. Dudley instantly ended up on the highlight-reel, for all the wrong reasons. This display is not just a showcase of power and skill; it carries a touch of pettiness, adding an extra layer of narrative to the unforgettable moment.

Shaq's dominance extended far beyond highlight-reel dunks. From his NBA debut in 1992 until his retirement in 2011, he stood as a colossus in the basketball world. Recognized as one of the top-10 players in The Athletic's NBA 75 list, Shaq's combination of size, strength, and basketball IQ made him the most dominant physical force of his generation. A member of the NBA's 50th Anniversary team in 1996, just four seasons into his career, Shaq's rapid ascent to greatness was a testament to his unparalleled skills and impact.

Championships are the ultimate currency of basketball greatness, and Shaq amassed a wealth of them. As the last true center to lead a championship team, he secured three consecutive NBA Finals MVPs from 2000 to 2002, joining the elite company of Michael Jordan. Shaq's impact wasn't confined to a single team; he guided the Lakers, Heat, and Magic to the grandest stages of the NBA. He wasn't just a player but the linchpin, the driving force behind title-contending squads.

Shaq's influence transcended the boundaries of basketball. Shaq's charisma and swagger were fresh air in an arena where big men often exuded an air of reservedness. His pursuits off the court showcased a multifaceted personality, demonstrating that he embraced the entertainment side of the business. Whether rocking the mic as a platinum-selling rapper, showcasing his acting prowess on the big screen, or engaging in philanthropy, Shaq's zest for life set him apart as a Renaissance figure in sports.

The end of his playing career did not signal a conclusion but rather a transition into a new phase of influence. Retiring from the court in 2011 only expanded Shaq's impact. He seamlessly transformed into a media personality, entrepreneur, and philanthropist. Collaborations with brands like Reebok, Pepsi, and Icy Hot showcased Shaq's versatility, while his media presence extended to TV shows, commercials, and even video games. Shaq's magnetic persona made him an ideal fit for various media platforms, earning him a substantial following.

The layers of Shaq's influence delve even deeper into the cultural fabric. Shaq also made his mark on pop culture with his appearances in movies, music, and even law enforcement, highlighting a diverse portfolio. Becoming a reserve police officer in multiple cities showcased a commitment to the community and a desire to make a positive impact beyond the basketball court. Shaq wasn't just an athlete—he was a cultural phenomenon, a living testament to the power of influence.

Shaquille O'Neal's life and career unfold as an epic tale, more than a mere basketball journey. Beyond his athletic prowess, charm, media presence, and diverse ventures, he has secured his place as a cultural marvel whose story continues to inspire and resonate with future generations.

INSPIRATIONAL QUOTES

"Excellence is a habit. You are what you repeatedly do."

"Everything happens for a reason. I'm used to it, I prepare for it. Like I say, at the end of the day, those in charge of their family."

"I really get motivated when I have doubters."

"Everybody talks about being a role model. But if you look up the word 'role' in a dictionary, it describes playing a part. Everything I'm into, it's real to me. There's nothing fake about it."

"To all the young people out there who think money and fame is important: that's only a small piece of the pie. You need an education to be totally secure in life. I feel very secure I can go get a real job now."

TRIVIA QUESTIONS

1. What nickname was Shaquille O'Neal commonly known by during his basketball career?

A) The Flash
B) The Diesel
C) The Jet
D) The Rock

2. In the iconic play against the New York Knicks on March 25, 1999, who did Shaquille O'Neal overpower before executing a thunderous dunk?

A) Michael Jordan
B) Charles Barkley
C) Chris Dudley
D) Kobe Bryant

3. How many consecutive NBA Finals MVPs did Shaquille O'Neal secure from 2000 to 2002?

A) One
B) Two
C) Three
D) Four

4. Apart from his basketball career, in which of the following areas did Shaquille O'Neal make significant contributions?

A) Law Enforcement
B) Culinary Arts
C) Space Exploration
D) Fashion Design

5. When did Shaquille O'Neal retire from professional basketball?

A) 2005
B) 2011
C) 2008
D) 2014

t Shaq's ability to transition from a dominant basketball player to a successful entrepreneur, media personality, and philanthropist emphasizes the importance of versatility and adaptability. Embrace change and be open to exploring different paths.

2. Perseverance in the Face of Challenges: Shaq faced numerous challenges throughout his career, including injuries and setbacks. His resilience and determination to overcome obstacles serve as a reminder to persevere in the face of adversity. Life is full of challenges; the key is to keep pushing forward.

3. Impact Beyond One's Field: Beyond his basketball prowess, Shaq's influence extended into various aspects of life, including entertainment, business, and philanthropy. This teaches us the value of making a positive impact beyond our immediate sphere of expertise, contributing to the broader community and society.

4. Embrace Diversity and Multifaceted Talents: Shaq's engagement in diverse activities, such as rapping, acting, and law enforcement, underscores the importance of embracing one's multifaceted talents and interests. Don't limit yourself to a single dimension; explore different passions and talents that contribute to your overall personal growth.

5. Cultivate a Positive and Charismatic Personality: Shaq's charisma and warm personality played a crucial role in shaping his success both on and off the court. Cultivating a positive attitude, being approachable, and spreading joy can create lasting connections and open doors to various opportunities in life.

Trivia Answers

1. B) The Diesel
2. C) Chris Dudley
3. C) Three
4. C) Law Enforcement
5. B) 2011

Dirk Werner Nowitzki, a legendary German basketball player, is not just a hoop star but a real global inspiration. Born on June 19, 1978, Dirk stands tall at 7 feet, making him one of the tallest power forwards ever. And, with 21 years of pure dedication to the game, all with one team, the Dallas Mavericks, Dirk has proved to be a loyal and dependable team member.

Dirk's got the stats that make your jaw drop—14-time All-Star, 12-time All-NBA Team member, and the first European player to bag the NBA Most Valuable Player Award. Oh, did we mention he's the highest-scoring foreign-born player in NBA history?

Dirk never imagined that he would lead his team to the NBA Finals, secure that elusive championship in 2011, and be named the NBA Finals Most Valuable Player. But before we get into that, let's start at the beginning.

As a boy in Würzburg, Germany, Dirk grew up in a sports-oriented family. Initially, he dabbled in handball and tennis before falling in love with basketball. Despite having a serious height advantage over his peers, Dirk faced challenges. Imagine being a towering teenager who felt like a "freak" for being so tall. But, not one to let his insecurities hold him back, he turned those fears into stepping stones, becoming an international basketball sensation.

Holger Geschwindner, Dirk's coach, saw his potential early on and crafted a unique training routine. It wasn't just about the game; it was about becoming a well-rounded individual. Training included playing a musical instrument and diving into literature to become a more complete person. Imagine playing with the best in the world or just being a local hero. Dirk chose greatness.

Fast forward to his professional career—a rocky start with the Dallas Mavericks, but Dirk's resilience shone through. He weathered the storm, learned the ropes, and soon became the team's cornerstone. The "Big Three" era with Steve Nash and Michael Finley marked a turning point, leading the Mavericks back to the playoffs after a decade-long drought.

Dirk's dedication and skill reached new heights in the 2002-03 season. He elevated his game and propelled the Mavericks to the Western Conference Finals. But, an injury to his left ankle kept him from giving it his all that season. Although they fell short, Dirk's performance would not be soon forgotten.

Off the court, Dirk's impact extended to the international stage, leading the German national team to bronze and silver medals in FIBA competitions. In 2023, he became the first German men's player to have his number retired—a testament to his global influence.

Dirk spent his entire 21-year NBA career with the Dallas Mavericks, a feat unmatched by any other player. He led the team to numerous playoff appearances, including a historic NBA championship in 2011. Dirk's scoring ability, versatile skills, and trademark fadeaway jump shot earned him the NBA Most Valuable Player Award in 2007 and the NBA Finals Most Valuable Player Award in 2011.

Following the Mavericks' 2011 NBA championship, the NBA faced a lockout that ended on December 8, 2011. The defending champions underwent significant changes in their roster, losing key players like DeShawn Stevenson, JJ Barea, Peja Stojaković, and Tyson Chandler. The team added new faces such as Lamar Odom, Delonte West, and Vince Carter. Despite a slow start and Dirk making his 11th consecutive All-Star appearance, the Mavericks finished seventh in the West. However, they were swept by the Oklahoma City Thunder in the first round of the 2012 NBA Playoffs.

Before the season, veterans Jason Kidd and Jason Terry left the Mavericks. Dirk underwent knee surgery, causing him to miss the initial 27 games. He returned in December 2012 and, along with his teammates, participated in the "Beard Bros" pact. On April 14, 2013, Dirk surpassed 25,000 career points, but despite their efforts, the Mavericks missed the playoffs for the first time in 12 years.

In January 2014, Dirk achieved the milestone of 26,000 career points. On March 12, 2014, he surpassed John Havlicek on the NBA scoring list, and on April 8, 2014, he moved to the 10th position, passing Oscar Robertson. The Mavericks reached the playoffs but were eliminated in seven games by the San Antonio Spurs, who eventually won the NBA championship.

Dirk re-signed with the Mavericks in July 2014. On November 11, 2014, he became the highest-scoring player born outside the United States, surpassing Hakeem Olajuwon. Throughout the season, Dirk continued to climb the scoring ladder, reaching several milestones, including his 10,000th career rebound. The Mavericks made the playoffs but were defeated by the Houston Rockets in the first round.

Dirk had notable performances during the season, including scoring his 29,000th career point. In the playoffs, the Mavericks faced the Oklahoma City Thunder and lost the series 4-1. This marked Dirk's final playoff appearance in his storied career.

In March 2017, Dirk achieved a historic milestone by becoming the sixth player in NBA history to score 30,000 regular-season points. Despite this individual accomplishment, the Mavericks missed the playoffs with a 33–49 record.

In 2017-18, he reached significant milestones during the season, including 50,000 career minutes and 31,000 career points. Unfortunately, he had season-ending ankle surgery in April 2018, and the Mavericks missed the playoffs. However, on March 18, 2019, he became the sixth-highest scoring player of all time, surpassing Wilt Chamberlain.

The postchampionship and final years of Dirk Nowitzki's illustrious NBA career are filled with remarkable milestones, achievements, and a heartfelt farewell to the game he dedicated over two decades to playing.

In an emotional ceremony during the final home game on April 9, Dirk announced his retirement, surrounded by basketball legends. The next day, he played his last NBA game, recording a double-double with 20 points and 10 rebounds in a loss to the San Antonio Spurs.

Dirk Nowitzki's final season marked the end of an era, and his impact on the game will live on in the minds of basketball enthusiasts all over the world. So, if you ever feel like the odds are against you, remember Dirk Nowitzki's story. Embrace your uniqueness, work hard, and shoot for the stars. Who knows? You might just create a legacy as remarkable as Dirk's.

INSPIRATIONAL QUOTES

"If you do the best you can, you have nothing to be ashamed of. A defeat is not a disgrace."

"I understand you've got to go through tough times to get better."

"All dreams are crazy. Until they come true."

"Success doesn't just happen overnight; it's a result of consistent hard work and dedication."

"I never focused on what I couldn't do; I always believed in what I could achieve."

TRIVIA QUESTIONS

1. What was Dirk Nowitzki's height during his basketball career?

A) 6 feet
B) 6 feet 8 inches
C) 7 feet
D) 7 feet 4 inches

2. In which year did Dirk Nowitzki lead the Dallas Mavericks to win the NBA championship?

A) 2005
B) 2008
C) 2011
D) 2014

3. Which prestigious NBA award did Dirk Nowitzki become the first European player to win?

A) NBA Finals Most Valuable Player
B) NBA Defensive Player of the Year
C) NBA Most Valuable Player
D) NBA Rookie of the Year

4. Which coach recognized Dirk Nowitzki's potential early on and implemented a unique training routine, including activities beyond basketball?

A) Rick Carlisle
B) Phil Jackson
C) Gregg Popovich
D) Holger Geschwindner

5. Dirk Nowitzki achieved the milestone of becoming the sixth-highest-scoring player of all time on March 18, 2019, surpassing which NBA legend?

A) Michael Jordan
B) Kobe Bryant
C) Wilt Chamberlain
D) Kareem Abdul-Jabbar

LIFE LESSONS

1. Embrace Uniqueness: Dirk Nowitzki's story reminds us to embrace our uniqueness. Despite feeling like a "freak" for being exceptionally tall as a teenager, he turned his differences into strengths and became an international basketball sensation. Embracing what makes you unique can lead to extraordinary achievements.

2. Resilience in Adversity: Dirk faced challenges and a rocky start in his professional career, but his resilience and determination shone through. Weathering storms and learning from setbacks are crucial to achieving long-term success. The ability to bounce back from adversity is a valuable life skill.

3. Dedication and Long-Term Commitment: Dirk's 21-year career with the Dallas Mavericks showcases the power of dedication and long-term commitment. Whether in personal or professional pursuits, staying committed to your goals over an extended period often leads to significant accomplishments.

4. Continuous Improvement: Dirk's coach, Holger Geschwindner, emphasized holistic training, including activities beyond basketball. This underscores the importance of continuous improvement, not just in one's primary pursuit but also in personal development. Being a well-rounded individual contributes to overall success.

5. Legacy and Impact: Dirk Nowitzki's impact extended beyond the basketball court, reaching the international stage and leaving a lasting legacy. The lesson here is to consider the broader impact of your actions. Whether in relationships, careers, or communities, the positive impact you make can contribute to a meaningful and lasting legacy.

Trivia Answers

1. C) 7 feet
2. C) 2011
3. C) NBA Most Valuable Player
4. D) Holger Geschwindner
5. C) Wilt Chamberlain

The Phoenix Mercury's rich history is filled with victories at the highest level and obstacles that were overcome with tremendous effort. Since their debut in 1997, they've evolved into a force to be reckoned with, clinching three WNBA championships in 2007, 2009, and 2014.

The early years under coach Cheryl Miller, a legendary baller herself, showed promise, with playoff appearances in the first two seasons. In 1998, the Mercury reached the league finals but fell short against the Houston Comets. However, changes in coaching staff and performance struggles, including a tough 8–26 record in 2003, marked a difficult period for the team.

Everything would begin to turn around under the guidance of then-owner Robert Sarver. The Phoenix Mercury was on the precipice of a pivotal transformation in 2004. This same year, Diana Taurasi was drafted and, two years later, Cappie Pondexter. This dynamic duo led the Mercury to a stellar 23–11 record in 2007, securing the top spot in the Western Conference. The team clinched its first championship by defeating the Detroit Shock in a thrilling five-game series. Pondexter's outstanding performance earned her the Finals MVP.

In 2009, with a 23–11 record once again, the Mercury claimed their second title by beating the Indiana Fever in a hard-fought series. With a scoring average of 20.4 points per game, Taurasi received both the regular-season MVP and finals MVP awards.

The subsequent departure of Pondexter in 2010 led to a dip in performance. Still, the team saw a resurgence in 2013 by adding 6-foot 9-inch center Brittney Griner. A former Baylor center and the first overall pick by the Phoenix Mercury, Griner's physical prowess was unparalleled. Griner embodied a new era in women's basketball with a wingspan surpassing Kevin Love's hands as colossal as Kareem Abdul-Jabbar's. Having witnessed her collegiate feat of 748 blocked shots, the league recognized the need for a defensive adjustment to prevent her from dominating the paint.

During the 2013 WNBA offseason, a meeting birthed the defensive three-second rule, a measure designed to curtail Griner's dominance in the paint. Even before she officially donned a Phoenix Mercury jersey, the rule had already earned the moniker "the Griner rule." A near-unanimous vote, with Phoenix as the lone dissenter, solidified the change, underscoring the impact one player could have on the game's landscape.

The parallels between Griner and other basketball legends who forced the game to change its rules were unmistakable. George Mikan forced the NBA to widen the lane; Wilt Chamberlain's athleticism necessitated further adjustments, including widening the lane to 16 feet; Abdul-Jabbar prompted the NCAA to ban dunking after his dominant sophomore season at UCLA.

Lisa Leslie, a WNBA legend in her own right, fittingly dubbed Griner as "Evolution." Leslie, a four-time Olympic gold medalist and the first WNBA player to dunk in a league game acknowledged that Griner had taken the game to a new level. Griner's impact wasn't solely about flashy dunks but her ability to defend the rim with unparalleled proficiency, forcing the league to adapt.

In her debut, Griner's two thunderous dunks captured headlines, showcasing her ability to play above the rim. The Mercury may have suffered a 22-point loss to Chicago. Still, the spotlight was undeniably on Griner, marking the beginning of her transformative journey in the league.

Griner, ever humble, recognized the learning curve and the need for continuous improvement. Guided by veterans Diana Taurasi and Alexis Hornbuckle, she embraced the opportunity to contribute to the game's growth. The conversation around Griner extended beyond statistics; it encompassed her potential to attract a new fanbase, making warm-ups exciting with her electrifying dunks.

Sandy Brondello took over as head coach in 2014, guiding the Mercury to a league-best 29–5 record and their third championship, with Taurasi earning her second finals MVP award. The team continued to excel, consistently making playoff appearances in the following years.

In 2020, Skylar Diggins-Smith joined the Mercury, adding to the scoring prowess alongside Taurasi and Griner. Unbeknownst to the basketball world, this era would witness the ascension of a legendary WNBA trio, soon to be anointed as the formidable "Big 3."

Skylar Diggins-Smith stepped into the spotlight, exhibiting strength, flexibility, and an extraordinary skill set. Following a hiatus due to pregnancy and the birth of her son in 2019, Diggins-Smith made an emphatic return, finishing the regular season ranked in the top 10 in scoring and assists.

However, it was her defining moment in the first-round playoff matchup against Washington that solidified her status as one of the league's great players. Diggins-Smith etched her name in Mercury history by leading an 11-point fourth-quarter comeback with 10 points and a game-winning assist. It was a message to her doubters that she had lost none of her brilliance during her missed 2019 season.

The stage was set, and as the years unfolded, Diana Taurasi, Brittney Griner, and Skylar Diggins-Smith would not only become integral to the Mercury's success but ascend to the echelons of the top 25 WNBA players.

As everyone geared up for the 2021 season, the anticipation and excitement were palpable, especially with ESPN's curated list placing the Mercury's iconic figure, Diana Taurasi, at a commanding No. 6. It was a testament to her enduring greatness that, at the age of 39, she entered her 17th season with a determined spirit. Her leadership was exemplified by guiding the Mercury to the playoffs for an astonishing 10th time, all while leading the team in scoring with an average of 18.7 points per game the previous season.

Alongside Taurasi in the upper echelons of ESPN's ranking were the Mercury's dynamic duo, Brittney Griner and Skylar Diggins-Smith, securing impressive positions at No. 13 and 14, respectively.

The 2021 season saw the team make another finals appearance, although they fell short to the Chicago Sky in four games. The trio of Taurasi, Griner, and Diggins-Smith elevated the Mercury's standing in the fiercely competitive landscape of the WNBA and solidified their places among the league's elite. Their collective narrative weaved together strength, triumphs, and a high basketball IQ, creating an enthralling saga that captivated fans and reverberated through the sun-drenched city of Phoenix.

Speaking of the city of Phoenix, the Mercury has become an integral part of the community. They're transforming the business game but not doing it alone. It's a team effort, and they're working with businesses that vibe with their values and believe in women's power.

These companies are not just big shots; they're the real deal, invested in the team and fighting for diversity, equity, and inclusion everywhere. Meet the Phoenix Mercury Changemakers! Imagine having Fry's Food Stores rocking the Mercury jerseys, PayPal adding some logo flair to the game uniforms, and Verizon being all over the practice gear. We're talking about some huge power moves. And it doesn't stop there. Bally's is making history as the first-ever market access deal with a women's team. It's a dream team, and they want more companies to jump on the bandwagon.

Taurasi can be found at the helm of some of the Mercury's new community initiatives. Her desire to fight for equality comes from her roots. She's not just speaking up for her family, who hustled to give her a shot—she's standing up for her teammates and friends facing a different world outside the gym.

Taurasi is a trailblazer using her platform to speak out against injustice. She feels it's her duty as the WNBA's all-time leading scorer to make sure you know where they stand. And let's keep it real—it's not always easy. Taurasi knows uncomfortable convos can ruffle feathers, but she's nct holding back. As she says, it's about bringing awareness and making the world better for everyone.

The Phoenix Mercury has laid a foundation of excellence that raises the bar. The team's resilience in overcoming obstacles, openness to change and evolution, emphasis on teamwork, and the leadership and mentorship exemplified by figures like Diana Taurasi illuminate paths to success in various aspects of life.

Beyond the basketball court, the Mercury's engagement in community initiatives and partnerships underscores the significance of social responsibility and advocacy. Their story extends beyond wins and losses, resonating as a source of inspiration, emphasizing the enduring power of determination, collaboration, and making a positive impact on the world beyond personal pursuits. The Phoenix Mercury serves not just as a sports team but as a beacon of strength, unity, and purpose, leaving an indelible mark on the hearts of fans and the broader community.

INSPIRATIONAL QUOTES

"Anybody that's different, be who you are. You never want to change that." - Brittney Griner, Center

"If I'm blocking shots or changing shots or even preventing players from taking shots, I'm helping the team and we are likely to win when our defense is playing well." - Brittney Griner

"Basketball is always evolving. You have to evolve with it. I'm not saying you should lose what you did in the past, but you just add to it, and it evolves." - Corey Gains, Head Coach 2006-2013

"If we have learned anything from the sacrifices and hard work from those that have come before us, it should be to celebrate proudly and help uplift others." - Candice Dupree, Power Forward

"There's a certain reason why certain people win because they have a winning mentality and they bring it into the locker room, into the gym every single day. You can't have enough of those people." - Diana Taurasi, Guard

TRIVIA QUESTIONS

1. Who earned the Finals MVP award in the Mercury's first championship win in 2007?

A) Diana Taurasi
B) Cappie Pondexter
C) Skylar Diggins-Smith
D) Brittney Griner

2. Which coach guided the Phoenix Mercury to their third championship in 2014?

A) Cheryl Miller
B) Robert Sarver
C) Sandy Brondello
D) Alexis Hornbuckle

3. What rule was introduced during the 2013 WNBA's offseason, often called "the Griner rule"?

A) Shot clock violation
B) Offensive three-second rule
C) Defensive three-second rule
D) Double dribble violation

4. Who is referred to as the "Evolution" by WNBA legend Lisa Leslie?

A) Diana Taurasi
B) Skylar Diggins-Smith
C) Brittney Griner
D) Cappie Pondexter

5. Which company is making history as the first-ever market access deal with a women's team?

A) PayPal
B) Bally's
C) Fry's Food Stores
D) Verizon

LIFE LESSONS

1. Resilience in the Face of Challenges: The Phoenix Mercury's journey, marked by early struggles and setbacks, showcases the importance of resilience. Despite facing difficulties, the team persevered, underwent transformations, and ultimately achieved success. This serves as a reminder that facing challenges head-on and staying resilient can lead to eventual triumph.

2. Embrace Change and Evolution: The introduction of the defensive three-second rule, dubbed "the Griner rule," emphasizes the impact of change and adaptation. Life constantly evolves, and being open to change, whether in personal growth or adapting to external circumstances, is essential for success.

3. Teamwork and Collaboration: The success of the Mercury's "Big 3"—Diana Taurasi, Brittney Griner, and Skylar Diggins-Smith—highlights the power of teamwork. Collaborating with others, leveraging individual strengths, and working toward common goals often leads to greater achievements.

4. Leadership and Mentorship: Diana Taurasi's role as a leader and mentor within the team underscores the importance of leadership in guiding others and fostering a positive environment. Whether in sports or life, being a supportive leader and mentor can contribute to personal and collective growth.

5. Social Responsibility and Advocacy: Taurasi's commitment to using her platform for social justice and equality reflects the broader concept of social responsibility. This chapter suggests that individuals have the power to make a positive impact beyond their immediate pursuits, advocating for meaningful change and standing up against injustice.

Trivia Answers

1. B) Cappie Pondexter
2. C) Sandy Brondello
3. C) Defensive three-second rule
4. C) Brittney Griner
5. B) Bally's

Unlock an even deeper appreciation for basketball with our exclusive free content: "100 Unique General Facts and Trivia Questions on Basketball." This resource is meticulously curated to enhance your understanding and enjoyment of the game. Whether you're a budding enthusiast or a seasoned fan, these facts and trivia questions will expand your knowledge, challenge your understanding, and provide hours of fun. Discover intriguing details about the sport's history, iconic players, and memorable moments that have shaped basketball as we know it today. To access this invaluable resource, simply scan the QR code provided and start your journey into the fascinating world of basketball trivia and facts.

CONCLUSION

As we reach the final buzzer, it's time to reflect on the incredible journey we've embarked upon—a journey filled with iconic stories of triumphs, setbacks, comebacks, and the unwavering pursuit of greatness. We've explored the heights and depths of basketball, witnessing legends emerge from every corner of the court.

From the undeterred spirit of Ben Wallace to the teamwork exemplified by the San Antonio Spurs, each chapter has been a testament to the power of passion, dedication, and the unyielding belief in oneself. The stories of Kobe Bryant, Diana Taurasi, and LeBron James have become echoes of inspiration, resonating far beyond the hardwood floors.

The Chicago Bulls of the 1990s and the Boston Celtics of the 1980s showcased the beauty of team cohesion and the relentless pursuit of excellence, setting benchmarks for generations to come. The dominance of the UConn Women's Basketball Team, the Minnesota Lynx, and the Phoenix Mercury in the WNBA has rewritten the narrative of women's sports, proving that skill knows no gender.

We've marveled at the unique playing styles of Kareem Abdul-Jabbar, Shaquille O'Neal, and Dirk Nowitzki, each leaving a permanent mark on the game. The underdog tales of Earl Boykins, Muggsy Bogues, and Giannis Antetokounmpo have taught us that greatness can arise from the most unexpected places.

The global impact of players like Yao Ming, who bridged the NBA with China, and the community contributions of teams like the Connecticut Sun and the Los Angeles Sparks, have showcased the transformative power of sports beyond the scoreboard.

So, as you close this book, let these narratives fuel your dreams, ignite your passions, and remind you that every challenge is an opportunity for a slam dunk into greatness. The game of basketball, with its ups and downs, its victories and defeats, is a mirror reflecting the stories of us all.